THE COMPLETE GUIDE TO
HOMEBUILT
ROTORCRAFT

D0878349

Dedicated to These Pioneers:

Juan De La Cierva, inventor of the Autogiro
Alexander Klemin, author of *Principles of Rotary Aircraft*
Igor Sikorsky, first American helicopter
Louis Breguet, first French helicopter
Dr. Heinrich Foche, first German helicopter
Chester Morris, author of *Pioneering the Helicopter and Test Pilot*
Benson Aircraft Corporation and Rotorway Aircraft, Inc., pioneers in the
    homebuilt rotary aircraft movement

THE COMPLETE GUIDE TO
HOMEBUILT
ROTORCRAFT

The essentials of
building and flying your own helicopter!

BY KAS THOMAS & JACK LAMBIE

MODERN AVIATION SERIES

TAB BOOKS Inc.

BLUE RIDGE SUMMIT, PA. 17214

FIRST EDITION

SECOND PRINTING

Printed in the United States of America

Reproduction or publication of the content in any manner, without express permission of the publisher, is prohibited. No liability is assumed with respect to the use of the information herein.

Copyright © 1982 by TAB BOOKS Inc.

Library of Congress Cataloging in Publication Data

Thomas, Kas.
    The complete guide to homebuilt rotorcraft.

    Includes index.
    1. Helicopters, Home-built. I. Title.
TL716.T48   621.133'352   81-18440
ISBN 0-8306-2335-3 (pbk.)   AACR2

Contents

Introduction

Man's earliest ideas of flight were always moving wings. The myths, such as the story of Icarus and Dedaelus, have them flapping their man-made wings vigorously as they made their escape over the sea.

The age of flight took a different direction when the Wright Brothers invented the airplane with fixed wings and propeller drive in 1903. Yet, Orville and Wilbur Wright began their fascination with flight playing with a toy rubber-powered helicopter given them by their mother.

Fixed-wing airplanes came to dominate aviation. The dream of human-powered flight was finally achieved with fixed wing and propeller drive instead of flapping or movable wings.

But the idea of moving the wing itself to generate lift was eventually perfected, and flying enthusiasts have a choice between fixed or whirling-wing aircraft.

The simplicity and convenience of flying with a set of easily handled and stored blades, of being able to quickly put the machine into the air after towing to a flying site has great appeal. The safety of slow landing and takeoff for rotary wing aircraft is outstanding when you consider that over half of their pilots had no previous experience before going into that type. The gyroplanes have fewer accidents per aircraft than any other airplane whether homebuilt or factory made.

The helicopter has realized man's dream of birdlike flight. It can go forward, back, up and down or even stand still like a hummingbird. Its wings are powered and move to create lift just like the bird except the blades spin, which is more efficient than the starting and stopping of birds' wings during each stroke. Of course, it's difficult to get veins and muscles to work in rotary style which is why creatures have feet and hooves instead of wheels.

The flashing blades of rotary aircraft generate a unique excitement. For any individual that treasures the thrill of moving through air with freedom and safety, this book gives a most complete primer to this wonderful world of a very special kind of flight.

Acknowledgments

The principal photographic contributor to this book was Wayne Thomas; other photographs were graciously supplied by Dr. Igor B. Bensen, Mr. Al Newell of RotorWay, Inc., Mr. Richard Cowan, and Mr. Gordon Doe. Special thanks go to these people, without whose help this book may not have been possible. Special thanks also go to Ken Brock, Marty Hollmann, RotorWay's George Pyszynski, Jim Eich, and Bob Dart for product information training manuals and photos; Irv Culver for gust discussions; Mark Lambie for patterns, and Fran Gionet for typing.

Chapter 1

How Rotarywing Aircraft Fly

When man created aircraft, he created them in two tribes: fixed-wing and rotarywing, in that order. Rotarywing devices still being in their infancy, they are not well understood by the general public—or even by the flying public. Most fixed-wing aviators don't know a gyroplane from wild hickory nuts.

So, before we begin to talk about the relative merits of homebuilt rotorcraft, let us first shed some light on rotorcraft in general: their classifications, background, aerodynamics, special vocabulary. "Define your terms!" the rhetorician shouts. And so we will.

Types of Rotorcraft

Rotorcraft, singular or plural, is a noun of general applicability to any flying machine that makes lift by means of one or more rotors (Figs. 1-1, 1-2). The two fundamental subclassifications of rotorcraft are *autogyro* and *helicopter*. Autogyro is an old term which, under pressure from the FAA, has given way to the newer word, *gyroplane*. Nonetheless, both autogyro and gyroplane are still used interchangeably. Gyroplanes of the homebuilt variety, moreover, are known as *gyrocopters*. (This is sometimes shortened to "gyro" in the interest of brevity.)

Helicopters, of course, need no introduction, the general public being familiar with such words as chopper, 'copter, helo, eggbeater, whirlybird, and so on.

Fig. 1-1. The Bensen B-12 "Magic Carpet" used ten engines of 7 hp apiece, driving ten two-bladed rotors. The unusual rotorcraft flew quite successfully and was capable of lifting an amazing 900 pounds.

The obvious question is: What makes a gyroplane, or autogyro, different from a helicopter? Aerodynamically speaking, how can they be told apart? The fundamental distinction is that a gyroplane's rotor system is unpowered, whereas a helicopter's rotor is engine-driven. The freewheeling rotor of an autogyro is always tilted aft in flight; this way, the oncoming air rushes up through the rotor, generating aerodynamic forces that keep the rotor turning like a child's pinwheel. By contrast, a helicopter's rotor is tilted *forward* in cruising flight and acts like a huge propeller, drawing the entire aircraft forward through the air.

Autorotation

The phenomenon of a rotor spontaneously turning as air rushes up from beneath it is known as *autorotation* (a word literally meaning "self-spinning"). A gyroplane's rotor is said to be in constant autorotation. Likewise, when a helicopter makes a power-off descent, its rotor is in autorotation.

Autorotation and windmilling are not exactly the same thing. In autorotation, the rotor blades fly at a positive angle of attack, while the blades of a windmill are "blown" around at a negative angle. A gyrocopter's rotor blades operate at about two degrees positive incidence; for larger gyroplanes, this value is often as high as seven degrees. How can a rotor whose blades are set at a positive angle keep turning? Aerodynamic forces make this possible, in the same way that a sailboat can make good a track that faces slightly into the wind.

Autorotation was discovered in 1919 by Juan de la Cierva, a Spanish inventor and aristocrat who experimented with model rotors in a wind tunnel. Cierva's work led, three years later, to the development of a novel aircraft which looked like a small monoplane with a rotor mounted on top. The rotor always turned in flight and prevented the craft from stalling.

Cierva called his creation the *Autogiro* (capitalized) and it turned out to be the world's first truly successful rotarywing aircraft, an accomplishment which brought Cierva the Daniel Guggenheim Gold Medal in 1932. (Harold Pitcairn, Cierva's American licensee, championed the cause of autogyros in the U.S. and received the Robert J. Collier Trophy in 1930.)

Gyroplanes of today are really much the same as the autogyros of the thirties. All modern gyroplanes have a single, unpowered main rotor for lift, and a conventional aircraft engine and propeller to provide forward propulsion. The rotor is always canted about twenty degrees rearward in order to capture oncoming air and keep the rotor turning. This makes controlled vertical descents possible,

Fig. 1-2. Although unconventional, the Bensen B-10 Prop-Copter with its synchronized, 72-hp McCulloch engines and short propellers must be considered a "rotorcraft." Differential vaning of thrust was used for control.

Fig. 1-3. Powered by a 70-hp Mercury outboard engine, the Bensen B-9 Little Zipster helicopter was extremely stable. One rotor turning one way and the other rotor turning the opposite way, no tail rotor was needed to counteract torque. Unfortunately, the small helicopter was never released in kit form and no plans are available.

but hovering is ruled out. Likewise, a runway must be used for takeoff and landing, although the landings are usually quite short—no more than a few yards.

Hovering

Helicopters, as mentioned, operate differently than gyroplanes because their powered rotors act like large propellers to create lift even while going nowhere. What this means is that helicopters—homebuilt or otherwise—can lift vertically and *hover* over a spot on the ground.

The precise way in which this is accomplished depends only on the ingenuity of the designer. But however it is done, the helicopter designer must face the fact that some method of *torque counteraction* has to be used wherever power is being applied to a shaft (Fig. 1-3). Any motion that is forcibly imparted to a rotor will, according to Sir Isaac, cause an equal but opposite motion to occur at the other end of the rotor shaft. What this says is that the fuselage of a single-rotor helicopter is going to want to spin opposite to whatever direction the rotor is spinning in. To prevent the fuselage from spinning counter to the rotor, most modern helicopters have a small sideways-mounted rotor at the tail end of the fuselage. This is the tail rotor or *anti-torque rotor*.

Gyroplanes, of course, have no need for an anti-torque rotor since the main rotor of a gyro is, in effect, wind driven. The only torque to be reckoned with in a gyroplane, as in an airplane, is the torque produced by the engine-driven propeller.

Rotor Terms

Rotarywing aircraft are so named because they have wings that rotate; these wings are called *rotor blades*. And in the same way that airplane pilots "fly the wing," rotarywing pilots "fly the rotor"—or the *rotor disc*, as it is frequently called (Fig. 1-4).

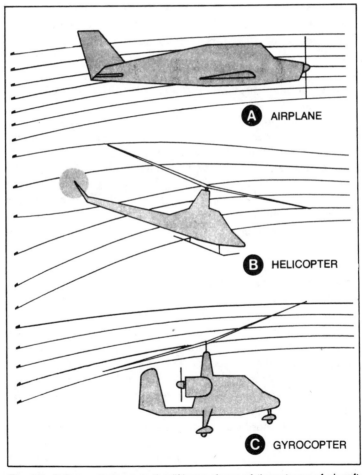

Fig. 1-4. Airflow patterns over the lifting surfaces of three types of aircraft: airplane, helicopter, and gyrocopter.

The rotor disc can be compared to an airplane's wing from another standpoint: that of *loading*. By analogy to wing loading, *disc loading* is defined as the weight of a rotorcraft divided by its rotor area. For a homebuilt with a rotor diameter of twenty feet, this number usually comes out to between 1.5 and 2.5 pounds per square foot. (For commercial helicopters, it can go as high as 10 pounds per square foot.) Disc loading has an important bearing not only on control response but on power-off sink rate as well. Machines with low disc loadings are generally blessed with quick control response and gentle power-off rates of descent. The opposite is also true: a ship with a high disc loading is going to fly like a bag of bricks.

Fixed-wingers often comment that the rotor blades of homebuilt gyrocopters and helicopters, which tend to droop some on the ground, look "too flimsy" or "too weak." There's more to this flaccid appearance than meets the eye, however. At flight rpm those slender blades become extremely rigid due to centrifugal force, which causes them to pull at the rotor hub with a force of some 7,000 or 8,000 pounds.

But because each blade is acted upon by several hundred pounds of lift as well as the enormous centrifugal force, the blades don't all fly in a flat plane; instead, they trace a cone (sort of like an inverted coolie hat). The extent to which the individual blades fly upwards is the *coning angle,* usually several degrees. The imaginary surface passing through the open part of the cone is called the *tip path plane,* a term that will be used again later on when discussing control movements.

Distribution of Lift

It's important to notice that since rotor blades travel in a circle, airspeed along each blade is not constant, but increases from root to tip. In other words, if a ten-foot-long rotor blade is being whirled around at 396 rpm, the tip of the blade will be flying at 400 feet per second, but the middle of the blade will only be experiencing an airspeed of half that, or 200 feet per second. When one considers that lift is proportional to the square of velocity, then it is evident that four times as much lift is produced at the tip of the rotor blade as at its middle. What this means in practical terms is that the outermost third of a rotor blade is the portion of the blade which makes most of the lift.

The foregoing holds true for the rotor of a ship that's sitting on the ground not going anywhere, but let's consider for a moment what happens when the rotor is moving through the air in cruising

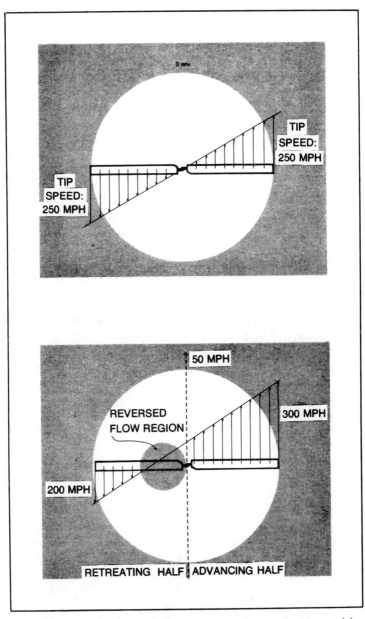

Fig. 1-5. Top left, a rotor is turning with a tip velocity of 250 mph while remaining stationary. Notice that the velocity varies along each blade, increasing from root to tip. On the bottom, we see what happens when the rotor is flying at a forward airspeed of 50 mph. Rotor blade velocity is no longer the same on both sides of the rotor, and part of the retreating blade is flying backwards.

7

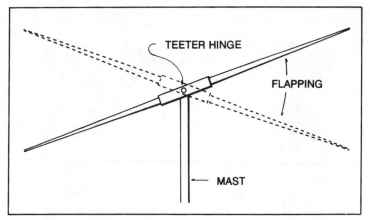

Fig. 1-6. A two-bladed, semi-rigid rotor system.

flight. Let's say the tip speed of our rotor is 250 mph—a reasonable figure for a homebuilt rotorcraft. But let's also say the whole rotor is moving through the air at 50 mph—also a reasonable figure. Obviously, on one side of the rotor disc the blades will be rushing to meet the oncoming 50 mph wind head-on, while on the opposite side of the rotor disc the blades will be traveling with the wind. What this means, simply, is that the blades on the upwind-traveling half of the rotor will experience a tip airspeed of 250 mph plus 50 mph, or 300 mph; while the downwind-moving blades will at one point experience a tip velocity of 250 *minus* 50, or 200 mph (Fig. 1-5). That's a 100 mph difference in tip speeds!

This difference in airspeeds between *advancing* (upwind-moving) and *retreating* (downwind-moving) rotor blades gives rise to an *asymmetry of lift.* That is to say, at any forward speed, one side of the rotor disc will produce more lift than the other side.

Note also that at any forward airspeed, the inboard portions of the retreating blades experience a *negative* airspeed. The area in which airspeed is negative is known as the *reversed flow region* and becomes increasingly larger with higher forward speeds. As this reversed flow region begins to devour a larger portion of each retreating blade, the remaining portion of the blade must work harder (that is, operate at a higher angle of attack) if it is to produce sufficient lift. The latter process can only go so far until the outboard portion of the retreating blade actually stalls from operating at too high an angle of attack. These two limitations—reversed flow and retreating blade stall—are the reasons that rotarywing aircraft have never been able to achieve fixed-wing aircraft speeds. In practice, this means that homebuilt rotorcraft are faced with about a 100 mph top speed limit.

Articulation

Returning to the problem of lift asymmetry, how is it that gyroplanes and helicopters stay upright and don't flip over in flight?

The answer has to do with the degrees of freedom allowed in rotor blade movement. The three basic degrees of freedom which can be incorporated into rotor systems are *flapping, feathering,* and *lead-lag* (in-plane movement). Flapping is the vertical, up-and-down movement of a rotor blade and is the key to equalization of lift on advancing and retreating halves of the rotor. By flapping upwards in response to its extra airspeed, the advancing blade disposes of its excess lift; by flapping downward, the retreating blade operates at a greater relative angle of attack and so creates more lift. Flapping forces are not felt by the aircraft, because the up and down movements occur around a *flapping hinge* at the root end of each blade (or a *teeter hinge,* in the case of a one-piece, two-bladed rotor).

Feathering movement allows the "pitch" or "incidence" of rotor blades to be varied. Axial movement of a blade about its spanwise axis is achieved through use of a *feathering bearing.* Most gyrocopters have non-feathering rotor blades that operate at a constant, fixed pitch.

Lead-lag or in-plane movement allows blades to speed up or slow down individually in response to Coriolis forces. This degree of freedom is only important in rotors with more than two blades. Thus, it is not important to builders of two-bladed gyrocopters and helicopters.

Types of Rotors

Depending on which degrees of freedom are employed in the design of the rotor head, three main types of rotors can be distinquished. When all of the above degrees of freedom are allowed, the rotor is said to be *fully articulated.* This is the case on most commercial rotorcraft with three or more blades. A rotor employing none of the above, or else feathering alone, is called a *rigid rotor* and relies on the flexibility of its rotor blades to accomplish the necessary flapping and lead-lag movement. The third main kind of rotor consists of a rigid hub supporting two rotor blades on a teeter hinge; this is the *semi-rigid* type of rotor that is used on virtually all homebuilts (Fig. 1-6). The semi-rigid configuration is by far the simplest and least expensive of the three rotor types (Fig. 1-7).

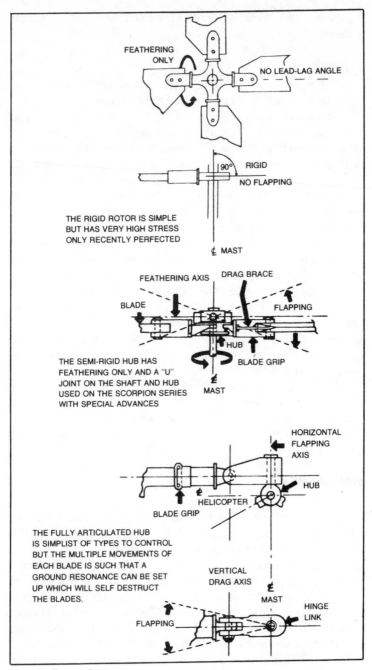

Fig. 1-7. Types of rotors.

Chapter 2
Gyrocopter or Helicopter?

"Nothing else equals it!" blasts one ad; "Answer to back-yard flight," another announces. "Easy to build," "Lowest cost," "Needs practically no maintenance," are some of the claims. Okay, so now you've read the ads, your eyebrows have hit service ceiling, and your heart joyfully palpitates at the thought of having your own whirlybird. But like most people, you aren't sure where to begin.

At this early state—when you have invested no money, your marriage is still intact, and your garage or apartment isn't cluttered with metal tubing and miscellaneous debris—this is the time to be thinking about what kind of rotarywing device best suits your purposes: gyrocopter or helicopter. Many people do not do enough thinking on this matter before sinking knee deep in nuts and bolts; if you doubt this, flip through a recent issue of *Trade-A-Plane* and note how many half-finished rotorcraft projects are up for sale. These are people who discovered too late that a Whirlygig-500 or Rotorfine II "wasn't right" for them.

Just as important as deciding whether to build a rotorcraft at all is the decision of whether to undertake construction of an autogyro or a helicopter. The considerations presented in this chapter are intended to help the amateur builder make this very personal decision.

Three Basic Machines

One might say there are three kinds of rotarywing designs on the homebuilt market: gyrocopter and helicopters (which we have already mentioned) and a third type, *gyrogliders*.

Gyrogliders actually do not comprise a unique rotorcraft category as much as a sub-category of gyrocopters, since a gyroglider is literally a gyrocopter without an engine. How does a gyroglider obtain forward airspeed—and so autorotation of the rotor—without benefit of an engine? By being towed continuously behind a car or truck.

In World War II, the Germans used gyrogliders as observation platforms, towed high behind U-boats. Also, the British investigated the possibility of using similar devices as rotarywing parachutes. After the war, General Electric in the U. S. conducted further investigations into the usefulness of kite-like rotarywing vehicles. Their test pilot was Igor Bensen.

The chief advantages of gyrogliders to amateur builders are as follows. First, gyrogliders are simpler and cheaper to build than any other rotorcraft. Controls consist solely of nosewheel steering for ground maneuvering, and a stick to tilt the rotor disc. Secondly, because they are extremely light and strong, most gyrogliders can lift several times their own weight; hence, they can tote two persons at once. This way, dual instruction can be given by an experienced pilot. The third advantage is that having learned to fly the gyroglider with comparative ease, the owner can at any time convert the ship directly to a powered gyrocopter by installing an engine and fuel system.

Gyrocopters and gyrogliders can be fitted with pontoons or floats and flown off of water, in which case they are called *hydrocopters* and *hydrogliders* (Fig. 2-1). Some have been fitted with skis for operation in snow. But regardless of the names given to these variants, there are only three kinds of rotorcraft for the amateur builder to consider. Since gyrogliders and gyrocopters, moreover, are so similar, and since most people who build a gyrocopter start with a gyroglider, what the prospective builder really must decide is whether he wants to build a gyro or a helicopter.

The Dilemma

The decision of whether to build a gyro or a helicopter should involve a handful of important factors, particularly the builder's need for an aircraft having a certain performance; the amount of time, money, and energy the builder is willing to invest in his project; and the piloting ability of the person or persons who are going to fly the finished product.

With regard to the first criterion, we have seen that autogyros cannot hover and must use a runway for takeoff; also, it so happens that most gyrocopter designs on the market are single-place. Obviously then, if a heavy load must be carried, or if true VTOL (vertical takeoff or landing) capability is required, a gyrocopter will not do.

On the other hand, a two-place helicopter is vastly more complex than a gyrocopter and costs at least twice as much to build. The average do-it-yourself helicopter project costs upwards of $20,000 and requires hundreds of man-hours of labor for completion. Thus, the builder must pay dearly for that extra little bit of performance that a helicopter offers. So it is easy to see that if paramount importance is placed on having an airworthy machine with as little a commitment of either time or money as possible, there's little alternative but to build a gyro. (Gyrogliders have been built in as little as one weekend.)

Then also, one must soberly consider the amount of time and diligent effort required to learn how to fly the finished machine. On this score, few people seem to realize how vast is the difference between learning to fly a gyroplane and learning to fly a helicopter.

Fig. 2-1. Put pontoons on a gyroglider and you have a hydroglider.

Probably anyone who could learn to fly a Piper Cub could learn to fly a gyroplane—after all, a gyroplane is a plane with a rotating wing. Helicopters, however, are a world apart. The torque control problems and new degrees of freedom experienced in helicopter flight make learning difficult, to put it tamely, for the beginner. Not only that, but an old adage among chopper pilots is *the larger the ship, the easier to adapt to.* Homebuilts, being at the small end of the scale, generally are not easy to adapt to, even for seasoned helicopter pilots.

Most pilots who fly both will agree that helicopters are more demanding to fly than gyroplanes; some argue that they are also more rewarding to fly. We'll talk more about the flying of these machines a little later on.

Uses and Non-uses

People are attracted to sport, or homebuilt, rotorcraft for different reasons. Some are lured by the low initial investment required. Others like the novelty afforded by building and flying "something different." Many fixed-wing pilots have turned to homebuilt rotorcraft in search of putting more fun back into their flying. These people are rarely dissappointed.

Some misguided souls, however, become involved with homebuilt rotorcraft with a view toward commuting to work—or worse, to the supermarket! To date, such mission profiles have not proven very feasible, for many reasons. Most beginners, for instance, fancy that they can take off in their gyrocopter from their back yard, when in reality their back yard would have to be a thousand feet long for this to be safely possible. Not only this, but city noise ordinances, federal minimum altitude laws, and restrictions on the flight of homebuilt aircraft over populated areas combine to make all but impossible *any* backyard takeoffs, no matter whether the machine in question is a gyrocopter or a pogo stick.

Some may develop their piloting (and public relations) skills to the point where they can fly a homebuilt helicopter to work from, say, the local airport, but even this assumes that the company allows helicopters to land on its roof or parking facility, and that the pilot and machine are compatible with the local airways system.

For the most part, homebuilt rotorcraft (like other homebuilts) exist for recreational educational reasons and lack utility value to all but a small number of exceptional individuals. The building and flying of small, do-it-yourself rotorcraft is a sport and should be thought of as such. To think differently is to invite disappointment.

Knowledge Is Power

For the budding hover-lover or gyro tyro, various sources of information exist which can be quite helpful in allowing the prospective builder to decide which project is "right" for him or her. One of the best of these sources is the advertising literature put out by the manufacturers themselves. Most of the large suppliers offer information packages ranging in price from $3 to $10. While these info packs are largely promotional in tone, they contain a lot of solid information on the company's products, the company itself, and even rotarywing flight in general (since these firms realize that most of the people reading their brochures are unfamiliar with rotorcraft). After reading several info packs, you'll not only know more about rotarywing aircraft, but you will also have some idea of which firms you would feel comfortable ordering critical components from.

Anyone who is at all serious about building a light rotorcraft should consider $20 or more spent on info kits and/or plans and drawings to be money well spent. The decisions you make after looking over these materials could have many important consequences. And at any rate, most manufacturers will refund the cost of info packs and plans on the purchase of components later on.

The serious-minded beginner would do well to join the Popular Rotorcraft Association, an organization similar in concept to (and about one-fifth the size of) the fixed-wing oriented Experimental Aircraft Association. Formed in 1962, the Popular Rotorcraft Association is a non-profit body "dedicated to the advancement of knowledge, public education, and safety" in the operation of noncommercial rotorcraft. In addition to hosting a large yearly convention and fly-in, at which seminars are given and trophies awarded, many of the P.R.A.'s fifty chapters sponsor local events and activities. Included in the annual dues of $18 is a subscription to the Association's bimonthly magazine, *Popular Rotorcraft Flying.* The P.R.A. can be contacted at P.O. Box 570, Stanton, CA 90680.

Gyrocopter Kits

Bensen. With more than 2,000 gyrocopters flying or close to flying worldwide—and well over 10,000 sets of plans sold—the archetypal Bensen B-8M has practically become an American institution (Fig. 2-2). Indeed, who could have read *Popular Mechanics* or any number of other magazines over the years and not seen an ad for the ubiquitous little copter?

Fig. 2-2. Bensen B-8M must use runway for takeoff and landing, cannot hover. Rotor is unpowered and always tilted slightly rearward in flight. Because rotor is wind-driven, no torque-correction devices are needed. Machine is capable of extended hands-off flight.

By any measure, this gyrocopter stands out as one of the outstanding aircraft designs of this century. This is especially true when one considers that at one time, a Bensen B-8M held 12 F.A.I.-sanctioned world records for speed, altitude, and endurance (Fig. 2-3); that several of Bensen's own prototypes are on display at the Smithsonian Institution Air Museum; that Bensen Aircraft Corporation lists among its past customers NASA, the FAA, the U.S. Army, Air Force (Fig. 2-4), and Navy, Cessna Aircraft, Lockheed Aircraft, Convair, Douglas, Goodyear Tire, and others; and that designers of other well-known rotorcraft (The Umbaugh 18 and RotorWay Scorpion, for example) started by building Bensen gyrocopters. Suffice it to say, without Igor Bensen's invention of the gyrocopter in 1953, there probably would have been no homebuilt rotorcraft movement as such.

Igor Bensen is the pioneer and founder of the homebuilt gyroplane movement. In 1939 he met his idol, Igor Sikorsky, the father of the helicopter, and followed in his footsteps. After working with General Electric as a research engineer and with Kaman Helicopter

Fig. 2-3. *Spirit of Kittyhawk,* a Bensen B-8M, at one time held twelve world records; it is now on display at the National Air and Space Museum.

Company as chief research engineer, in 1953 he began development of the Bensen gyrocopter (Fig. 2-5). In 1962 founded the popular Rotorcraft Association and was president for ten years. It now has membership of over 14,000.

Aviation Consumer Newsletter found that Bensen gyrocopters had 0.3 percent fewer accidents per machine than all other amateur-built aircraft. This is remarkable considering that 60 percent of Bensen pilots had student licenses or none at all.

Fig. 2-4. The Bensen B-80 was tested by the U.S. Air Force.

Fig. 2-5. Igor Bensen's first gyroglider weighed only 62 pounds and cost $100 to build in 1952.

The Bensen gyrocopter is the most popular homebuilt flying machine ever with over 4,000 built. Bensen publishes a newsletter, *Flying News,* filled with articles on construction, safety, and activities. He has been working on his latest gyrocopter which uses a semi-powered rotor so there is less problem with blade stall; much shorter takeoffs can be made, since there is no need for a long run to spin up the rotor.

One notable difference between the Bensen and other gyroplanes is the mounting of the control stick directly on the hub so that it comes down from above. This makes it very light and simple but is different than the action most power pilots use. For hang glider pilots it is identical in that weight shift (or rotor tilt) is actuated by moving the control opposite to the way you wish to go. Push forward to climb, pull back to go down, hold to the right to make a left turn, and left for a right turn.

Most Bensens use the 72-hp McCulloch engine and this type holds most of the FAI World Gyrocopter speed records. Bensen kits can be purchased by part starting at $1,750 to $2,695 for the glider trainer models and $4145 for the B-80 kit (Figs. 2-6, 2-7).

Bensen Aircraft Corporation,
P. O. Box 31047,
Raleigh, NC 27622.

Brock. Ken Brock has flown homebuilts for over 25 years and was a Bensen dealer. He flew from California to Kitty Hawk, North

Carolina, in ten days in 1971. As a plant manager for an oil field instrument company, he was experienced in advanced machine work. Gradually he refined the systems on his Bensen by adding a

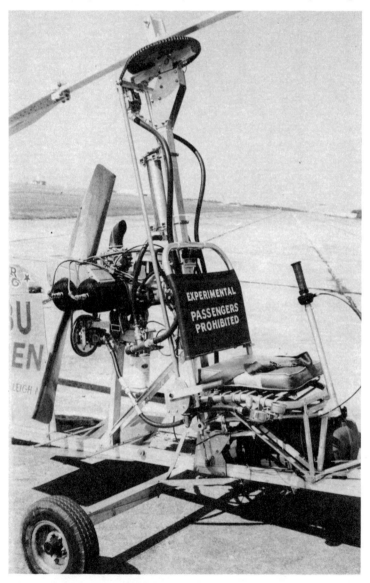

Fig. 2-6. This Bensen has the standard controls and a flexible shaft belt-driven rotor drive for pre-rotating. Note the throttle on the stick and FAA required "experimental" sign on the seat.

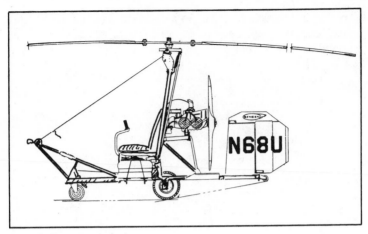

Fig. 2-7. Bensen gyrocopter.

standard control system, custom high-strength wheels with roller bearings, and superbly finished lightweight parts (Fig. 2-8).

Brock remains friendly with Dr. Igor Bensen and still uses rotor blades from the Bensen factory. The KB-2, however, has a special engine mount, a large aluminum rudder, and a patented fuel tank seat.

Ken Brock Manufacturing has 22 full-time workers making parts for the gyroplane and many other type of homebuilt airplanes. The glider kit is $2395. The power accessories kit at $1205 includes everything but the engine. The plane uses the popular McCulloch

Fig. 2-8. Ken Brock demonstrating his KB 2 gyrocopter using a McCulloch engine. Note the airspeed indicator just to the left of the nose (the pilot's right).

Fig. 2-9. The HA 2 Sportster, two-place gyrocopter by Marty Hollmann.

4318GX engine. The engine and propeller are $1700 extra. A converted Volkswagen can also be used ranging from $800 to $3500 depending on options. Many KB-2 builders have opted to use the Revmaster engine with the turbocharger which gives outstanding power at high altitude and on hot days. The Revmaster is available from J. Horvath at Chino Airport, Chino, California for $3500.

Fig. 2-10. The HA 2 uses a 150-hp aircraft engine.

Ken Brock Manufacturing
11852-P Western Avenue
Stanton, CA 90680

Gyrocopter Plans

Hollmann. Marty Hollmann is a very qualified Lockheed structural engineer who was born in Germany and came to the U.S. after WWII where he earned his Master's Degree in mechanical engineering at Florida Tech. He formed the International Gyroplane Association to bring together interested gyroplane builders from all over the world. He sells three plan sets and you can get the complete information package for $10.

Winther-Hollmann Aircraft, Inc.
11082 Bel Aire Court
Cupertino, CA 95014

HA-2M Sportster. The Sportster is a two-seater side-by-side enclosed gyroplane that can fly between 28 and 90 mph. When the rotor is prespun, the plane will take off in only 350 feet.

Marty became interested in gyroplanes and noted that no two-place ships were available, so he developed the Sportster. His gyroplane shows meticulous detail design for strength and simple construction. It uses a standard aircraft engine, the Lycoming 0-320 of 150 hp, to give it a cruise speed of 65 mph.

The assembly is designed for the homebuilder with few tools. The aircraft is bolted together of square aluminum tubing using aircraft nuts and bolts. The plexiglas windows are hand bent, of single curvature, and pop riveted in place.

The builder can make his own rotor blades of aluminum or spend $1250 for the special laminar flow blades. These laminar blades enable the craft to fly with half the power of the conventional aluminum type. Marty has calculated that the new laminar blades will, for a 600 pound gyroplane using a 65-hp engine, increase speed 5 mph, range 50 miles, and rate of climb 300 fpm.

Cost to build the craft in 1978 was $8918.50 not including tools, machining, or welding. About two years of spare time work, or 1500 hours, is required to complete the project.

It can be towed to and from the airport on its own wheels by a hitch on the rear bumper of a car. The Sportster has been towed coast to coast with no problems. The blades were stored in a box on the roof of the car.

This craft, the HA-2M Sportster, uses a collective pitch mechanism and a pre-rotator that engages the engine to spin the blades at 240 rpm. This results in a much shorter takeoff run. For taxiing on narrow strips or roads and to protect the blades, a rotor brake is used to keep the blades aligned fore and aft (Figs. 2-9 through 2-12).

Blueprints, assembly instructions, and maintenance manual are $150.

Fig. 2-11. Dual controls of the HA 2.

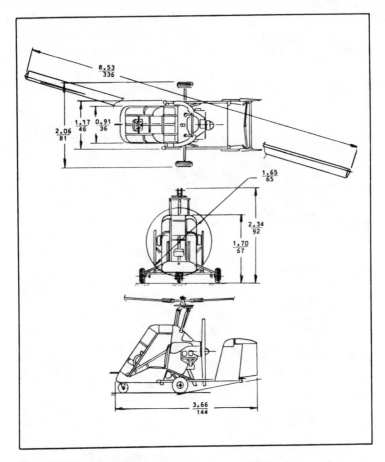

Fig. 2-12. HA 2 Sportster.

John Bond Sky Dancer. The Sky Dancer (Fig. 2-13) uses welded steel tubing instead of the square aluminum of the Bensen and Brock machines. It uses the 2100 cc Revmaster Volkswagen engine with a Troyer propeller to create 375 pouunds of thrust. The empty weight is 280 pounds, and gross weight 540. It climbs 1200 fpm and can take off in only 150 feet after the rotor is spun. It uses conventional joystick controls. Plans are $58.

J4B Gyroplane. This is a single-seat gyroplane with a welded steel tube. Using a 100-hp engine, its minimum speed is 40 mph and maximum speed is 115. Featuring shock absorbers on all three wheels of the landing gear and 4130 steel tubing it is strong and crash resistant (Figs. 2-14 through 2-16).

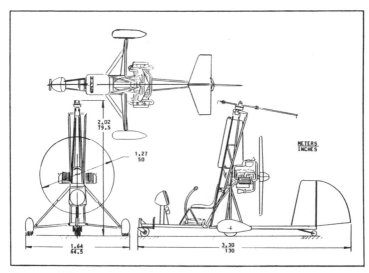

Fig. 2-13. John Bond Sky Dancer.

Helicopter Kits

International. In 1954 Harold Emigh, an aeronautical engineer at North American Rockwell, designed a homebuilt helicopter based on the best technology of the time. It used a 150-hp Lycoming aircraft engine and welded steel tube construction. Many

Fig. 2-14. The Barnett J-4 gyroplane is rugged, comfortable for long trips. Ship features fiberglass enclosure, Continental engine.

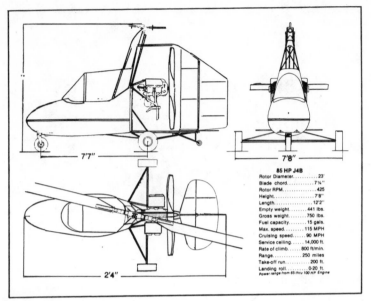

85 HP J4B	
Rotor Diameter	23'
Blade chord	7¼"
Rotor RPM	425
Height	7'8"
Length	12'2"
Empty weight	441 lbs.
Gross weight	750 lbs.
Fuel capacity	15 gals.
Max. speed	115 MPH
Cruising speed	90 MPH
Service ceiling	14,000 ft.
Rate of climb	800 ft/min.
Range	250 miles
Take-off run	200 ft.
Landing roll	0-20 ft.
Power range from 65 thru 100 HP Engine	

Fig. 2-15. Barnett J-4.

of his single-seaters were built and flown successfully, and a two-place was introduced in 1969. It was called the Helicom (Figs. 2-17, 2-18).

Having a 25 year history operating all over the world, it seemed a good product for Bob Dart who acquired the entire operation and moved it to his factory in Mayville, New York.

Fig. 2-16. Barnett J-3M, an earlier version of the current J-4 model.

Fig. 2-17. The Helicom Commuter Jr. shown above is the design of Harold Emigh, whose other famous design is the all-metal 1948 Trojan tricycle-gear airplane. The Commuter, powered by 150-hp Lycoming, can hover at 5,800 feet with two passengers and 16 gallons of fuel. It is now offered by International as a kit for $15,000 to $20,000 with many improvements.

The new Commuter was developed from the old Helicom. The craft now has 25-foot blades, 2 feet longer than the older version, a far more streamlined and stylish cockpit, and many other improvements (Figs. 2-19, 2-20).

Fig. 2-18. The International Commuter Jr. copters have steel trusswork tail, use shafts and gearboxes, and are powered by Lycoming and other aircraft engines.

Fig. 2-19. International 1982 Commuter II kit is 1950s technology.

The more complicated components are assembled at the factory, then sent to the buyer to bolt into the frame. These include main rotor transmission, tail rotor gearbox, main rotor blades, tail rotor blades, main rotor head and grip assembly, and the clutch assembly. These "necessary" kits to build the Commuter and can be gotten only from the company at a cost of $9651 (1982).

If you wish, you can buy the airframe tubing and other parts at an aircraft supply store or by judiciously picking up surplus items from various airports. The company will, however, supply these parts (airframe kit, fuel tank kit, etc.) for $3861.

Then, if you really want a lot of the craft ready for assembly, they will furnish the welded airframe, exhaust system, and gas tanks for another $1750. The 150-hp Lycoming engine can be found in fairly good condition for $3000 to $5000. Total cost for the complete helicopter kit is $20,000.

The company publishes a newsletter, *The Commuter Commenter,* with a permanent mailing list charge of only $10. It lists builders, and experiences of those who have completed their machines. Safety maintenance hints and up-to-date modifications are included.

International Helicopters
P. O. Box 107
Mayville, NY 14757
Telephone: (716) 753-2113

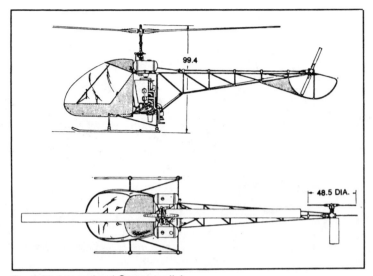

Fig. 2-20. International Commuter II-A.

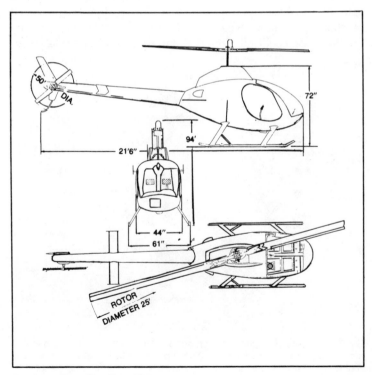

Fig. 2-21. RotorWay Executive.

Fig. 2-22. The RotorWay Scorpion employs belts and pulleys to drive main rotor and tail rotor. Price is on a par with a new sports car.

RotorWay. RotorWay began experimenting with a small helicopter in 1961 and consistently improved its performance and reliability. It is now recognized as one of the most advanced and complete homebuilt kit aircraft of any kind ever marketed.

Fig. 2-23. Details of engine, radiator, and belt drive system are visible is this photo of a partially-completed Scorpion (that which belonged to the author). Engine is 135-hp Johnson outboard. Machine is on trailer for easy road transport.

Fig. 2-24. Scorpion rotor head is of the semi-rigid teetering type, underslung on two pivots at right to each other. Cyclic pitch change is actuated through a pushrod that moves in response to a swashplate; collective pitch is controlled by cable which runs up through rotor shaft and attaches to small walking beam as shown.

Fig. 2-25. RotorWay's Scorpion carries two.

31

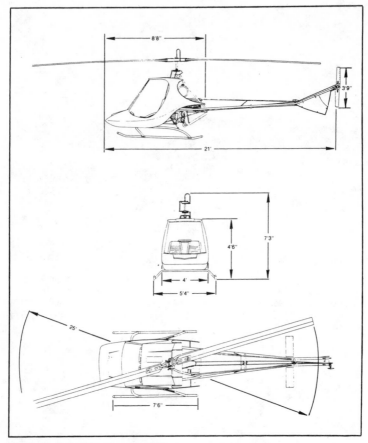

Fig. 2-26. RotorWay Scorpion 133.

The latest version, the two-place Executive (Fig. 2-21) developed from the earlier Scorpion, uses their own liquid-cooled engine which allows minimum cooling drag and safe temperature under any condition. The plane has a combination structure of 4130 steel tubing frame, aluminum monocoque tail boom, and streamlined fiberglass pilot enclosure.

The rotor is turned by a two-stage reduction system. The first stage is a V-belt which can slip slightly during startup to absorb torsional vibration. Second stage is a chain drive to provide high torque transfer with little power loss.

RotorWay has recently developed a new nonsymetrical rotor blade airfoil which slowed its engine off descent rate by 50 percent to ensure safer landings.

The company emphasizes a "one step at a time" procedure. First, study the plans. Then order parts unit by unit. Using tools such as drill press, metal-cutting band saw, and welder, the craft is completed in 500 hours spare time.

After construction, a one week hover training session is conducted at RotorWay's plant in Arizona. The builder is given instruction in preflight, maintenance, weight and balance, rotor system tuning, and cockpit procedures. They teach the builder to fly in one of RotorWay's own training ships, so it is not even necessary to bring a helicopter. The builder practices at home with his own helicopter only what has been learned in the training sessions so far. Next, the builder brings his own helicopter to the factory for advanced training and final advice on checkout and maintenance. This training is included in the kit price!

The kit is very complete and factory assistance and support so thorough that 80 percent of builders have completed their machines.

Each group of the assembly runs from $2000 to $7000 so the builder can purchase each section and begin construction without an immediate massive outlay.

The Scorpion 133 (Figs. 2-22 through 2-26), with a useful load of 220 pounds and a cruise speed of 80 mph, costs $21,445; the Executive is $25,874. Options such as dual controls, carpeting, custom upholstery, can add another $1500.

RotorWay Aircraft Inc.
14805 South Interstate 10
Tempe, AZ 85284

Chapter 3

Construction

Happily, most do-it-yourself rotorcraft projects require less building time and ability than most fixed-wing projects. A person who wouldn't dream of trying to build a Pitts Special or Thorp T-18 is usually capable, of building a gyrocopter. Mechanical aptitude, in other words, is rarely a major problem in the construction of a small helicopter or gyrocopter (Fig. 3-1).

What most newcomers lack is the basic information needed to get them started: namely, what supplier to order from, what tools are going to be needed, what costs to expect, how to take care of registration and other paperwork . . . in short, "What am I getting into?" That's what we'll talk about right now.

The Cost Factor

Of all the reasons people are drawn to homebuilt rotorcraft, low cost seems to head the list. Gyrocopters, for instance, are practically within anyone's budget; gyrogliders are even less expensive. About the only thing cheaper to build would be a hang glider.

This has caused its share of problems, both for the rotarywing sport and for hang gliding. As if properly constructed aircraft were not inexpensive enough, some overzealous types resort to the use of "reject" hardware (such as when electrical conduit is used in the control system—an extreme example, but a true one), thus concocting an aircraft that can only properly be referred to as "junk parts

34

flying in formation." The sport's safety record suffers as a result. The moral should be obvious: *when your life is at stake, don't let cost considerations interfere.*

We have already mentioned the fact that of the rotorcraft available to homebuilders, gyrogliders are cheapest to build. What this means in dollars and cents is that you can expect to shell out about $2500 for a safely-constructed gyroglider—give or take some, depending on how many prefabricated parts are employed (Fig. 3-2). Next come the gyrocopters, which are gyrogliders plus engine, fuel system, throttle, and instrument panel. Depending again on how many prefab assemblies are used in construction, anywhere from $4000 to $6000 can reasonably be spent on a one-

Fig. 3-1. A rotorcraft can be built in a small space.

Fig. 3-2. Precision machining is the name of the game in the fabrication of gyro rotor head parts shown here. Most builders buy their rotor head as a factory-finished item.

man gyrocopter. One and two passenger helicopters are a quantum jump higher on the price ladder and start out at about $20,000. This price includes many factory-finished items (rotor blades, for instance) that cannot be made by the amateur builder. You won't be far wrong if you equate the cost of a gyrocopter to that of a small economy car, and the cost of a helicopter to that of a popular sports car.

To the above costs, figure an additional $900 or more for a trailer to transport the finished product to and from the flying area, and several hundred dollars for radio if you intend to operate from a tower-equipped airport. Custom paint jobs and accessories, of course, are still more.

Hourly costs, when one considers fuel, oil (which two-stroke engines use in grandiose quantities), maintenance, taxes, storage, insurance (if any), and cost of driving to and from the practice area, can be $20 for gyrocopters and even more for helicopters. Bear in mind, this says nothing about the value of one's own time spent in labor; while we're at it, figure in about a half hour of maintenance and inspection time for every hour of flight time for a helicopter, and not much less for a gyrocopter. This is in line with the best that commercial rotorcraft operators can achieve, incidentally.

These are rough figures, representing an average around

which there is bound to be considerable fluctuation. However, these figures should be given careful consideration by anyone seriously contemplating a rotarywing homebuilt. If the numbers sound too high, maybe hang gliding really *was* the sport you were interested in after all.

Design Considerations

As said before, the choice of whether to build a gyro or a helicopter should be predicated on many considerations, among them such factors as the minimum performance desired, money available, and the skill and patience that one is willing to devote to learning how to fly. Building time is another consideration, for while you may finish a gyrocopter in only 100 man-hours, you'd be hard put to spend less than several times this figure completing a two-place helicopter.

One's building capabilities should also be given some thought before embarking on what may be too demanding a project. (Of course, you can always buy a machine that someone else built—but then, do you trust their workmanship any more than you do yours?) Unless the seller has receipts, how will you know what quality of hardware was used in the craft's construction? And why is the person selling the ship in the first place? Is it because he's afraid to fly it himself?) If you are going to build a gyroglider or gyrocopter, you will need to use at least the following tools:

☐ A hacksaw.
☐ A set of files.
☐ A mallet.
☐ An electric drill.
☐ Wrenches.
☐ Pliers.
☐ Screwdrivers.

These tools will get you through the construction of a Bensen B-8 *if* you purchase some prefabricated items (such as a factory all-metal tail). There is considerable leeway in time and ability required to complete a Bensen gyro depending on how many pre-cut, pre-drilled, or prefabricated items are employed in construction. This gives rise, in turn, to substantial fluctuation in building costs, since factory-finished components are quite a bit more expensive than the raw materials.

If, on the other hand, you've decided to undertake construction of a helicopter, you will need not only the above basic tools but also

Fig. 3-3. Welding skills are needed to build a small helicopter. Airframe of Scorpion shown here is constructed of chrome-moly steel. Plans for single-place version of Scorpion are no longer offered by RotorWay.

an acetylene welding torch, a drill press, and occasional access to a machine shop—or "farm out" many components and assemblies (Fig. 3-3). Again, some items may be purchased prefabbed from the factory. The FAA has the final say over how many so-called factory "kits" (pre-finished items) can be used in a rotorcraft project, since current regulations require that the builder supply 51% of the man-hours necessary for completion of the ship.

The person who decides to construct a gyrocopter will find that he basically is limited to building a Bensen, or else something that looks similar to a Bensen except for the Eich JE-2 (Fig. 3-4), there are no tractor-configuration, old-style autogyros on the homebuilt market, for instance. One of the more original gyroplane designs available to the homebuilder is the J-4 gyro. This machine boasts a fully-enclosed fiberglass cockpit, welded steel tubing airframe (in contrast to the bolt-together aluminum Bensen frame), and power supplied by 75-hp and larger Continental aircraft engines.

The helicopter scene lay dormant until just a few years ago; now, however, hundreds of homebuilt helicopters are in flight status across the U. S. At this time, the two major contenders for helicopter business are International Helicopters and RotorWay, Inc. International's one and two-place Commuter Jr. designs utilize shafts and gearboxes in main and tail rotor transmissions, and can accept Franklin or Lycoming aircraft engines. RotorWay's popular Scorpion Too, in contrast, utilizes belts and pulleys to transmit power to the rotors. (This is nothing new: the Hughes 300 copters use V-belts also.)

Regardless of whether a gyro or a helicopter is being considered, one may rest assured that large and reputable firms exist which offer time-proven designs. Bensen Aircraft Corporation and RotorWay, Inc., for example, are members of the National Association of Sport Aircraft Designers and adhere to NASAD's guidelines in the selling of plans and parts. Therefore, unless the builder is a graduate aeronautical engineer with experience in rotorcraft design, *no attempt should be made to design a wholly original homebuilt rotorcraft, be it gyrocopter or helicopter.* The designing of a rotorcraft is a serious business, and shouldn't be entered into by amateurs. Not when proven designs exist.

Paperwork

Homebuilt rotorcraft, like all civil aircraft in the U. S., must carry at all times a registration certificate as well as a valid airworthiness certificate.

The first can be obtained simply by appearing in person at the local General Aviation District Office (GADO) of the Federal Aviation Administration. (Look under Dept. of Transportation in the U.S. Government section of the phone book.) Ask for a registration application. You'll be given a form to be filled out in triplicate; two copies will go to the FAA headquarters in Oklahoma City along with

Fig. 3-4. James P. Eich's JE-2 gyroplane is of tractor configuration.

a modest registration fee. The extra, pink copy is your temporary registration certificate, which should be stowed aboard your ship. Within 90 days of mailing your application to the FAA, you will receive a permanent copy of the registration certificate along with an 'N' number assignment. The 'N' number must be painted in six-inch tall, block-style letters and numbers on the rudder of your machine. The deadline for this is the first-flight date; it would be wise to make application for registration at least 90 days in advance of the anticipated first-flight date.

Airworthiness certificates for civil aircraft are issued under several categories: normal, utility, restricted, limited, experimental. All amateur-built aircraft have to be licensed under the Experimental category. This means, among other things, that the word EXPERIMENTAL must be painted in two-inch letters on or near the craft's cockpit where it will be clearly visible. That's what the rules say.

To obtain an airworthiness, certificate, the rotorcraft must meet with the approval of an FAA inspector or designee. In the case of most gyros and helicopters, this can be taken care of in one shot by arranging for an inspection with the GADO sometime in the final weeks of construction. It's good practice to let the FAA know well in advance of completion that you're building a Bensen B-8 or whatever; don't expect them to come out and issue an airworthiness certificate the day of your first test flight. Once an appointment has been made by phone, the GADO will send an inspector out to your shop or garage to inspect the nascent whirlybird for part defects, poor construction or design practices, bad welds, and such. If all is deemed okay, an Experimental Category Airworthiness Certificate will be issued immediately and test flying may begin.

None of the foregoing applies to gyrogliders, which the FAA consigns to the kite kingdom. Kites are exempt from all paperwork under current Federal Aviation Regulations. However, if tow-releases are to be made, or an engine mounted, *then* the above considerations with regards to registration and airworthiness *do* apply.

In addition to the above, there are special restrictions put on the operation of homebuilt aircraft, fixed- and rotary-winged, that the builder-pilot should know. For example, once licensed as airworthy, an amateur-built aircraft is restricted for the first 75 hours of flight to operation within 25 miles of a designated test site or practice area. (If the aircraft uses a standard aircraft engine, such as a Lycoming, the "test" period is 50 hours rather than 75.) Each

GADO is prepared to assign a test site within reasonable range of the builder's home, so that the builder won't have to travel immense distances in order to fly. However, during the 75 hour break-in period, *all* flying must be done within a 25 mile radius of the practice field, and *no* other airports can be operated from without prior authorization. Cross-country flights to other airports are, in other words, forbidden.

During the 75-hour test period, no flying can be done over populated areas, and even after the 75-hour limit, no flights may be conducted in IFR (instrument flight rules) conditions, at night, or for compensation. Not only that, but if any part of the aircraft is changed or modified during this period (say a larger fuel tank is installed) the airworthiness certificate becomes invalid and a new 75-hour test period begins. To make the airworthiness certificate valid, the GADO must be contracted and another airworthiness inspection arranged.

If all of this sounds petty and mean, bear in mind that exceptions to the rules can be and frequently are granted. For instance, the GADO will normally grant a written waiver of regulations to allow a person to take his new whirlybird to a fly-in or other get-together away from the practice area. Waivers are also granted to allow flight over congested areas. If you have a need to bypass a certain rule or restriction, petition your local GADO for a waiver. They'll be happy to talk it over with you.

Options, Accessories, and Modifications

Homebuilt aircraft in general are noted for their individuality and creative workmanship. This is no less so for homebuilt rotorcraft. Substitutions of engines, fuel systems, control systems, rotor systems, and customization of prop spinners, instrument panels, pilots' seats, and a zillion other items, combine to make each and every gyrocopter or helicopter thoroughly unique (Figs. 3-5 through 3-10).

Many design modifications and substitutions are superfluous or trite—the use of many unnecessary switches and dials on instrument panels, for instance. Other mods are quite serious.

One choice that the builder of a gyrocopter or gyroglider will want to confront early in construction is whether to use an overhead (azimuth-type) control stick, or a between-the-knees joystick. This is a highly personal decision, of course, but those who have been exposed to lightplane flying will probably prefer the joystick. The operation of a joystick is simple: push forward to go down, push

Fig. 3-5. Among the options clearly visible in this photo are a sleek fiberglass body enclosure and custom protective covers for rotor head and prop.

right to go right, etc. The azimuth-type stick is standard equipment on Bensen products and is mechanically simpler than a joystick, but it is more difficult for some people to master. The reason is that to go left using an overhead stick, one must lean to the *right* on the stick, thus causing the rotor disc to tilt to the left. This kind of rotor control was popular with some of the early helicopter designers,

Fig. 3-6. The extra weight of a cockpit fairing can result in over ten percent less power requirement due to less drag.

Fig. 3-7. Bensen with a twin snowmobile engine drive on skis for winter flying.

notably Stanley Hiller Jr., but is no longer promoted by anyone except Bensen. If you drive your car with your hands at the bottom of the steering wheel, the overhead stick is probably right for you. Otherwise you may want to use the joystick. It's up to you.

Another important decision the builder of a gyro should confront is whether or not to build wooden rotor blades. If the idea of using wooden blades registers with you like fingernails scraping a chalkboard, consider that for many years the early helicopters flew with wooden blades—in fact, some autogyro blades were builtup

Fig. 3-8. This helicopter features a fully-sealed cockpit for operation in minus twenty degree weather in Minnesota.

Fig. 3-9. Some builders go all out on instruments, as shown here. This Barnett J-4's panel features cylinder head temp gauges, altimeter, ASI, engine tach, oil and fuel pressure and oil temperature gauge. At top is magnetic compass, fuel gauge, ammeter. Machine uses dual-ignition aircraft powerplant, has electrical system.

like airplane wings, using wooden ribs and doped fabric covering. Even the relatively modern (ca. 1966) Air & Space 18-A gyroplane, which was commercially mass produced, employed blades having a laminated spruce leading edge and a balsa trailing edge covered with resin. So suffice it to say there is nothing inherently unsafe about the use of wooden rotor blades. However, the builder is still faced with the choice: build his own wooden blades relatively cheaply, or spend $500 or more for a set of ready-to-use metal blades.

This is, again, a highly personal decision which may be dictated in part by the financial resources of the builder. But while the wooden rotor blades offer an initial advantage in cost, it must be pointed out that wood has one very significant drawback: it warps. Wooden blades are very sensitive to conditions of temperature and humidity. In addition, the non-uniform nature of wood makes it virtually impossible to build two rotor blades that are completely alike. What this means is that wooden blades are harder to trim and operate less smoothly than aluminum blades over their useful life. For hassle-free operation, metal blades can't be beat. But if the blades strike an object or are damaged in handling . . . ouch! There goes $650—$1250.

Related to rotor blades is the subject of *pre-rotators*. A pre-rotator is a device which is used on a gyrocopter to mechanically pre-spin the rotor blades to near-flight rpm just prior to takeoff. The alternative to pre-rotators is simply not to use one, in which case the rotor blades must be hand-propped to 50 or 60 rpm before taxiing, and then aerodynamically accelerated to higher rpm during the taxi run. Some gyro owners tire of the "Armstrong" method of starting up the rotor and seize upon the first opportunity to install a one or two horsepower motor to pre-spin the rotor. However, most gyrocopters do not have pre-rotators.

One of the most controversial of design substitution questions is that of which engine to use (Figs. 3-11 through 3-13). The argument is the old one of which is better, a two-stroke engine or an Otto-cycle (four-stroke) engine? It is a fact that most homebuilt gyrocopters and helicopters flying today use high-pollution, ear-piercing, and (some say) tempermental two-stroke engines. Why? The answer is simple enough. No other kind of engine available to amateur builders puts out as much punch for so few pounds of weight. Power-to-weight ratio for a rotorcraft is crucial. Hence, it doesn't make sense to equip a 200 pound gyrocopter with a 200

Fig. 3-10. Floats are a popular conversion. The hull on this ship is experimental, made of fiberglass. Photographed at Oshkosh, 1972.

Fig. 3-11. McCulloch 4318 GX is standard on Bensen gyrocopters. Advantages are light weight and good power output—90 hp. Contrary to popular misconception, these engines do not come from drones but are bought new or remanufactured.

Fig. 3-12. Volkswagen engine is no longer a rare sight on gyrocopters. A typical installation is shown here. Belt reduction to prop allows the propeller to turn slower, work more efficiently.

pound aircraft engine that delivers 100 horsepower, when an 86-pound McCulloch 4318GX engine will put out 90 horsepower. The Outboard Marine Corporation engines used in Scorpions end up weighing more, since they are water-cooled, but the principle is the same.

For those who disdain the use of "two-bangers" in anything but lawnmowers, there are gyrocopter and helicopter designs which incorporate standard aircraft engines. Barnett gyros use 65-hp and

Fig. 3-13. Recognize the engine? It's a Honda, 750 cc. Experimental rig develops marginal thrust, even with prop reduction. Other engines—Porsche, Hirth, Franklin, Continental—have also been tried on Bensen machines.

Fig. 3-14. In June of 1971, Ken Brock of Anaheim, California, flew this gyrocopter coast-to-coast in ten days. This photo was taken in Jackson, Tenn. Flight began in Long Beach, ended at Kitty Hawk.

75-hp Continentals, for instance, and the Commuter Jr. copters can take 125-hp Franklins or 150-hp Lycomings.

The question always arises: Why not use a Volkswagen engine? It's been tried; indeed, after years of debate on the subject, Bensen Aircraft Corporation has relented to print conversion plans for equipping B-8 gyros with VW engines. Based on years of cumulative experience using the VW engine, it now appears that this engine can be used with success on lightweight gyrocopters for normal sea-level operations. That is, under conditions of normal low density altitude, the VW engine offers sufficient power reserves to allow an adequate margin of safety for most types of operation. On hot days or at high altitudes, however, the performance just isn't there.

Still, the argument continues, four-cycle enthusiasts maintaining that two-stroke engines are "too unreliable" for use on flying machines. Two-stroke enthusiasts are just as likely to disagree. I myself believe that a two-stroke engine having properly-gapped and seated plugs, and a fully-functional magneto, is just as reliable for most uses as any Otto-cycle engine. When Ken Brock of Anaheim,

California flew coast-to-coast on his Bensen gyrocopter in ten days, he experienced no mechanical difficulties with his 90-hp McCulloch. I know—I was part of the support crew for that trip (Fig. 3-14).

The important rule to remember, regardless of the choice of engine, is that for a gyrocopter to have adequate performance the static thrust (in pounds) produced by the engine and prop turning at full rpm must be equal to or greater than half the gross weight of the ship. In other words, a gyrocopter weighing 520 pounds at takeoff must be able to produce 260 or more pounds of static thrust at full throttle. (This would be about average for a 72-hp McCulloch 4318AX engine. Well-maintained 90-hp McCullochs turning a 48-18 prop have been known to produce 325 pounds of thrust at sea level.)

It would be possible to go on for dozens of pages talking about variations in fuel systems, instrument panels, cockpit enclosures, wheel pants, rotor brakes, and the myriad other things that go to make up a rotarywing homebuilt. But by now the reader has no doubt gotten the picture. Although plans and drawings may look cut and dried, there's actually much room for experimentation—which is what those little two-inch letters are all about on or near the ship's cockpit.

Chapter 4
Pilot's Licenses

A frequently-asked question is: Do you need a pilot's license to fly a homebuilt gyrocopter or helicopter? The answer is *yes*; both the machine and its pilot must be licensed to fly. For the aircraft itself, this means having and carrying an airworthiness certificate, and for the pilot it likewise means being appropriately certificated. No aircraft, homebuilt or store-bought, can be flown without a license, and that includes small gyrocopters and helicopters.

Pilots who obtained their private license in a fixed-wing aircraft should realize, however, that their license entitles them to fly anything except jets or heavy aircraft, *solo*. That means that anybody who holds at least a private license—regardless of the original rating—may solo a homebuilt gyrocopter or helicopter. The only time a rating is needed is when passengers are to be taken, and that goes for any kind of aircraft—even blimps.

A few pages ago, it was mentioned that the FAA considers gyrogliders to be kites. This means that gyrogliders need not be registered or certificated as airworthy, and it also means that gyrogliders may be flown with impunity by unlicensed novices. However, if tow releases (free flights) are to be made, then the gyroglider must be registered and certified as airworthy *and* the pilot must be licensed.

What kind of license is needed in order to fly a homebuilt rotorcraft? The minimum license necessary would be a student pilot's license. The applicant for a student pilot's certificate must be at least 16 years of age; the first step in obtaining this permit is to make an appointment with an FAA designated Aviation Medical Examiner for a Third Class physical exam. These examiners are usually general practitioners in the community who have been approved by the Federal Air Surgeon to act as Aviation Medical Examiners. (There will no doubt be one near you; try the phone book or call the local FAA Flight Standards Office.) When you appear for the physical, be prepared to fill out a medical history questionnaire and an application form which you will sign and which will later become your flying license. First, though, you'll submit to a thorough medical exam, which can cost upwards of $30.

The exam itself is fairly routine and takes roughly a half hour. The doctor will be looking for such things as good color vision, at least 20/50 vision uncorrected or else 20/30 corrected, the ability to hear the whispered voice at three feet away, blood pressure within a healthy range, no prior history of drug addiction, epilepsy, alcoholism, diabetes, etc.

In case you're wondering, only a little more than one percent of all applicants are denied their medical certificates. Interestingly enough, the most common grounds for denial involves not visual acuity, but cardiovascular problems. Only about eight percent of Class Three failures are due to eyesight difficulties.

Assuming you pass the medical exam, you will be granted your Third Class Medical Certificate before leaving the doctor's office. This certificate doubles as a student pilot's license when it has been validated on the reverse side by a Certified Flight Instructor.

Before validating a student pilot's certificate, a CFI is required by Federal Aviation Regulation (FAR) 61.87 to determine, first of all, that the applicant is familiar with the flight rules of FAR Part 91 as they apply to student pilot's, and secondly that the applicant has received instruction in flight preparation procedures, including pre-flight inspection and powerplant operation, and ground handling and run-ups; in addition, the person must show an instructor that he can make three successful *towed* flights if the person intends to fly gyrocopters. This accomplished, the CFI affixes his name to the reverse side of the medical certificate, indicating the type of aircraft to be flown by the applicant. The student pilot may then fly *only* the type of aircraft indicated (Bensen B-8M, for example). The certificate is then good for two years, after which the entire procedure, beginning with a new medical examination, must be repeated.

In the meantime, the student pilot may not carry passengers, or fly for hire or in furtherance of a business; nor can he or she attempt cross-country flights, or flights to strange airports, unless the flight instructor has appropriately endorsed *both* the student pilot's certificate and the pilot's logbook.

So as you can see, student pilots are subject to a plethora of restrictions. Nonetheless, for many homebuilt rotorcraft enthusiasts, obtaining a student pilot's certificate in their machines is the easiest and cheapest way to get in the air.

Eventually, the builder-pilot may want to earn a private pilot's certificate with either a gyroplane or helicopter rating, as appropriate. It bears emphasizing that such a certificate *must* be obtained if passengers are to be taken up in a two-place design. The prerequisites for obtaining a private license are as follows. The applicant must be at least 17 years old, be able to understand English, and currently hold a valid Third Class Medical Certificate; in the case of a helicopter rating, the applicant must have logged at least 15 hours of solo time in helicopters, with an additional 25 hours of dual time in aircraft, including a takeoff and a landing at an airport serving both airplanes and helicopters, a flight with an off-airport landing, and three hours of cross-country flying. In the case of a gyroplane rating, the applicant must have logged 10 hours of solo time in gyrocopters and an additional 30 hours of solo and dual instruction in aircraft, including flights with takeoffs and landings at both paved and unpaved airports, and three hours of cross-country flying. Also, the applicant must have received instruction in various ground and air operations as set forth in FAR 61.107 (Flight Proficiency). The final requirements are that the applicant achieve a grade of 70 percent or more on the appropriate FAA written test, and pass a flight test with an oral examination.

According to FAR 61.45, the applicant for a private license (or for an additional rating to be added to a private license) may, at the discretion of the examiner, furnish an aircraft for the flight test which has *only a single seat or set of controls*. In this case, the examiner may direct the applicant to perform certain maneuvers and then observe these maneuvers from the ground or from another aircraft. If this procedure is followed, the license or rating which is issued will be appended by a note limiting the applicant to solo flight ony. The usual procedure, of course, is to have the flight examination conducted in a two-place aircraft—in which case the license which is issued will bear no restrictions on the number of passengers that may be carried.

If these rules seem detailed and involved it's because they are. For that reason, and because the rules are constantly being changed, it would be a smart idea for the reader to pick up a copy of the latest FARs from the local airport bookstore and study them.

Getting a pilot's license is not difficult; it *does* require patience, perseverance, and training. But obtaining a license in the manner outlined here can be quicker—and less costly—than the usual routes, especially when a helicopter rating is sought. Only joining the Army would be more expedient!

Hang gliders have not been required to have a license as long as they were able to be foot launched. With the advent of powerd hang gliders, and the increased danger of trying to foot launch, the FAA has proposed new rules to create a special class of aircraft that need not be licensed, nor will their flyers need a pilot's certificate. It may have a great impact on the sport of rotor flying.

The rules limit weight to 154 pounds (70 kilograms) but there is great pressure to move this to the world standard of 100 kilograms for the special class. This new weight, if adopted, will, at 220 pounds, come very close to the empty weight of the Bensen and Brock machines.

Being able to fly without the bureaucratic *nonsense* of a flight physical, licensing, use-taxes, etc., may well bring another surge in the development and flying of the new class of ultralight rotorplanes!

Chapter 5
Flying the Gyroglider

If you can't afford a gyrocopter or a helicopter, or if you simply want to sample rotarywing flight before investing in a powered ship, or if you want to build and fly a rotorcraft without the red tape and expense of becoming a licensed pilot, then you could hardly go wrong by building a gyroglider. Because no license is needed, there are no age restrictions. All kinds of people have flown gyrogliders, including eleven-year-old kids, grandparents in their seventies, even paraplegics. The hands-off stability of most gyrogliders makes them excellent confidence-builders for persons who have never flown anything before. And you can't beat the price: the only thing cheaper to build and fly would be a hang glider.

The gyroglider is an excellent training device for pilots wishing to transition to powered gyrocopters, since a gyroglider is a gyrocopter without an engine. The only relatively safe way for a would-be gyrocopter pilot to train for powered flight is to check out first in a gyroglider (Fig. 5-1). The way current Federal Aviation Regulations are written, an aspiring gyrocopter pilot *must* demonstrate to a flight instructor his ability to safely fly a towed gyro before his student pilot's certificate will be endorsed for solo powered flights. Thus, not only common sense but federal edict make it mandatory for a gyro tyro to start out in gyrogliders.

What follows is not intended to be used as a syllabus but is provided only to acquaint you with the various aspects of gyroglider flight. If at all possible, seek dual instruction from a qualified pilot before attempting to solo either the glider or the copter version. Most Bensen dealers and P.R.A. chapters are equipped to give glider check-outs. If instruction is *not* available near where you live, adhere to the Bensen manual when teaching yourself how to fly. *Follow a plan* and do not deviate from it; overconfidence will be your number one enemy.

Preparations

Until some experience is gained, it would be prudent to use a towline of no more than fifty feet (Fig. 5-2). Towline in this case means 1000-pound test manila rope, or ¼ inch steel cable. Nylon rope is elastic and acts like a rubber band; use it if you want. You'll always want to make extra sure there are no cuts or frayed areas along the rope or cable and that the cable is securely fastened to the car or truck's tow hitch. This does *not* mean tying the rope around the bumper.

For all tow runs it will be necessary to have a straight, open, level area free of obstructions, potholes, kids, motorcycles, etc., and pointing squarely into the wind. The wind velocity is unimpor-

Fig. 5-1. By virtue of their light weight, gyrogliders can take two passengers. Machine shown here is traveling 35 mph.

tant if the wind is steady and not gusting. In fact, if the wind is strong enough, you can dispense with the two vehicle and simply lash the gyro to a tree or other sturdy object. This way, you can practice flying while remaining stationary over the ground, a practice known as "kiting."

The tow vehicle should be driven upwind as necessary to take out any slack in the towline before operations begin. From that point on, no towline slack should ever be allowed to occur.

Naturally, before towing begins it's imperative that the driver of the tow vehicle knows exactly what is expected of him or her. (It goes without saying that the driver must be mature, conscientious, and responsible. *Know your driver.*) Communications signals should be worked out so that the driver can adapt to any given situation. The signals commonly in use are as follows:

1. Pilot's left arm fully extended, thumb pointed up, means "begin towing" if the run is just starting, or "increase speed by 5 mph" if the run has started.

2. Pilot's left arm extended, thumb pointed down, means "slow down."

3. Same as '2' except with up-and-down motion of arm means "It's time to land," to which the driver responds by simply letting his foot off the accelerator. (At no time should the driver apply brakes.)

4. Pilot's fingers moved back and forth across neck: "End of run; let's come to a full stop." This signal is given on the ground, after landing.

Fig. 5-2. Normal relationship of gyroglider to tow vehicle—either car or truck—is shown in this photo.

The driver should carry one passenger in the vehicle to act as a safety rider who will always keep an eye on the pilot and be ready to interpret signals. No other passengers should be allowed.

Ideally, the driver should be a gyroglider pilot also, or at any rate be familiar with principles of gyroglider flight. The driver should realize, for instance, that *airspeed* is what counts to the pilot, not speedometer indications. An airspeed indicator can and should be mounted on the tow vehicle.

No instruments are required on gyrogliders. Nonetheless, it would be foolhardy not to have at least an airspeed indicator. Conventional ASI's are not sensitive enough in the gyro's speed range, so most gyroglider and gyrocopter pilots buy and use the little "windspeed indicator" that looks something like a thermometer and has a tiny "pith ball" that slides up and down a glass tube to indicate velocity. These devices are inexpensive and can be obtained from most gyrocopter dealers.

Starting the Rotor

When ready to start, one should don a good helmet, clear the immediate area of spectators, and begin to pre-spin the rotor blades by hand if no pre-rotator (see Chapter 3) is available. To do this, stand in front of the axle on the left side of the ship; with your left hand, move the joystick forward to bring the blades within easy reach, and use the right hand to reach up and grab a rotor blade from behind, close to the hub bar. Start the rotor turning clockwise, looking from below, always pushing against the same part of the blade: the trailing edge near the hub. Continuing in this manner, "pat" the rotor to at least 50 rpm or so. Then, without undue delay, sit down and buckle yourself in the pilot's seat and signal the driver to start (thumbs up).

If you've ever wondered how a gyrocopter's rotor starts turning, that's how. In the old days (ca. 1930) a long rope was wound around the autogyro's rotor shaft and a contingent of bystanders was enlisted to heave-ho. I've seen pictures of small, blade-mounted rockets being used to start a gyro's rotor. Today's large gyroplanes, such as the McCulloch J-2 or HA-2M, use a helicopter-like transmission to supply power directly from the engine to pre-spin the rotor before take-off. During takeoff, of course, the transmission is disconnected so as to leave the rotor freewheeling.

Once the driver has seen your thumbs-up signal, he will slowly accelerate to between 5 and 10 mph and wait for your next signal.

Fig. 5-3. Ground steering is accomplished by guiding castoring nosewheel with feet; braking action occurs by pressing with heels on square of plywood which rubs tire. Rudder pedals are not needed for normal gyroglider operations.

During this time, the rotor (if pre-spun to at least 50 rpm) will respond to the oncoming airflow by maintaining and then increasing rpm. If, however, the rotor was not pre-spun to an adequate rpm, or if the driver accelerates too quickly, the blades will not accelerate in rpm. Instead, the large "reversed flow region" created over the retreating half of the rotor will cause the blades to flap downward and hit the teeter stop, and this will be felt in the stick as a two-per-revolution (2-per-rev) knock or vibration. This vibration can become severe and knock the stick from the pilot's grip. Corrective action consists of signaling the driver to reduce speed and pushing forward on the joystick.

Not much steering has to be done in a gyroglider, but it is important to make steering corrections as necessary, to keep the machine in a straight line behind the tow vehicle (Fig. 5-3).

Assuming no problems have been encountered, the rotor should stabilize at around 120 rpm a few seconds after reaching 10 mph. Once rotor rpm has stabilized, a thumbs-up signal should be given to the driver; the driver will smoothly accelerate to 15 mph. After half a minute or so at the new speed, the rotor will have picked up additional rpm and will again reach a plateau. Then it's time to give another tumbs-up signal, whereupon the driver will accelerate to 20 mph. This step-wise increase of speeds is necessary to allow the rotor to gradually increase rpm without flapping against the teeter stop. It takes time for the rotor to reach to a higher airspeed by turning faster; you can't hurry the rotor.

When about 25 mph has been reached—slightly higher if the glider is carrying two persons—the rotor will accelerate into the flight-rpm range. Several cues forewarn the pilot of this. One is that the joystick will acquire a new feel as aerodynamic forces on the blades are fed back into the pilot's grip. Also, now that significant lift and drag are being produced by the rotor, the entire machine will seem to want to rock back onto the tiny tailwheel; forward stick will, in fact, be required to keep the nosewheel from leaving the ground. An aural cue is also afforded by the loud slap-slap-slap of the rotor when it reaches flight rpm. As the pilot receives and interprets all these cues, he should neutralize the stick, give thumbs-up, and be prepared to break ground.

Liftoff

Just prior to levitating, the gyro may roll a short distance on its main wheels alone. This poses no problem other than the fact that steering control is temporarily lost. The important thing is not to attempt to steer using the control stick, as this could cause the machine to dart sideways on liftoff, or even roll over.

The final bit of acceleration from takeoff speed (near 25 mph) to flight speed (35 mph) can be quite brisk without risking rotor flap,

Fig. 5-4. On takeoff, gyroglider will break ground near 25 mph. This machine has been registered, as evidenced by N-number on tail, and already carries engine mounts. Note tiny tail wheel.

since considerable centrifugal force is now acting on the rotor blades. (If the driver knows this in advance, time and runway space can be conserved.) When the machine is accelerated past takeoff speed, it will rise off the ground smoothly and without pilot effort; the stick will still be in the neutral position. The pilot is now flying (Fig. 5-4).

Because there are no rudder controls or throttle, all maneuvering is done with the control stick. Assuming a joystick is used, one need only push forward to lose altitude, push left to go left, etc. The pilot will find that while the control stick is not "touchy," nonetheless very small control movements will always do the job. Constant control pressure in the desired direction of flight is unnecessary; it's only necessary to give an initial nudge of the stick in the desired direction to send the machine floating off gently in that direction. The control response differs somewhat depending on whether wooden or aluminum blades are used. The wooden blades typically have a longer control lag and are harder for the novice to adjust to. This is because control inputs are delayed, through flexure of the blades, in reaching the blade tips; thus, the tip path plane changes only slowly. By contrast, aluminum blades are much stiffer and provide immediate control response.

Most pilots who have flown the gyroglider will agree that it is one of the easiest of all homebuilt aircraft to fly. To prove the point, some years back Bensen engineers took a standard B-8 gyroglider equipped with an offset gimbal head (Fig. 5-5), loaded it with ballast, and flew it behind a truck with *no* pilot. The machine took off, remained behind the tow vehicle, and landed with only the assistance of an expert tow driver. Several such flights were made in this way, not just one.

Landing

At all times during the tow run, the pilot should be aware of where the end of the road or runway is and how soon to begin thinking about landing. Gyroglider landings can be accomplished in fairly short distances; nonetheless, all landings must be well thought out in advance, with ample runway space allowed.

Upon deciding to land, the pilot should bring his ship straight behind the tow vehicle, if he hasn't already. This centered position should be maintained throughout the landing maneuver—otherwise the craft will touch down in a crabbed position, which can be hazardous.

Next, the pilot should apply forward pressure on the joystick as required to bring the machine to within one or two feet of the ground. Sudden, jerky movements of the stick must be avoided, for if the stick is hastily shoved forward, slack can develop in the

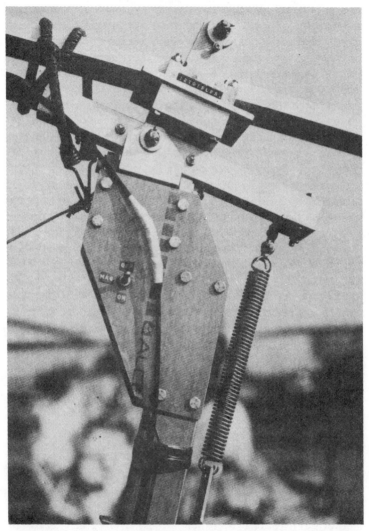

Fig. 5-5. This is the offset gimbal rotor head used on most gyrocopters of the Bensen type. Hub bar is underslung several inches from the teeter bolt. Springs at rear of rotor head are ground adjustable for pitch trim. Note magneto switch on cheek plate.

towline. (If slack should develop, curse yourself and be prepared for a jolt when the slack is taken up. This is but one of many reasons why you should always wear a helmet.) Again, remain directly behind the tow vehicle. When coming to within inches of the ground, a cushion of air will form between the rotor and the ground, which in turn will impart extra rpm to the rotor. The excess rotor rpm will make the ship seem buoyant and the pilot will have to keep the machine near the ground with forward stick pressure.

Now is the time to give the first thumbs-down signal. When the driver or safety rider sees the pilot very close to the ground giving this signal, both the driver and the observer should know that the pilot wants to land. The driver should react by letting his foot off the accelerator. (Remember, no brakes! And if a stick shift is used, avoid sudden decelerations.) A constant, steady deceleration to 10 or 15 mph will result in the glider's having nowhere to go but down. All the pilot will have to do during this whole time will be to flare slightly so as to touch main wheels first. Otherwise, the ship will land itself.

If there is room for another flight, the pilot can at this point signal thumbs-up and a smooth acceleration all the way to 35 mph should cause no blade-flapping problems. If the pilot wishes at this point to end the run, he signals the "cut" motion with his fingers across his neck.

Free Flights

It was mentioned earlier that in order to attempt free flights with a gyroglider, both the gyro and the pilot must be licensed. That means, the ship must carry registration and airworthiness slips and an 'N' number on the tail, and the pilot must possess at least a student pilot's license which is properly endorsed. Only if these prerequisites are met can tow releases be performed.

Tow releases are not normally made by the average gyroglider enthusiast; normally, all flights will begin and end with the towline attached. Upon hearing the word "gyroglider" for the first time, many people automatically assume that the craft is, indeed, some sort of glider. A gyroglider *can* glide, but it cannot soar. Pilots who perform tow releases generally do so either to improve their flying ability in anticipation of transitioning to powered gyrocopters, or to bring added fun and excitement to their gyroglider operations (Fig. 5-6).

Prior to performing tow releases, a thorough weight-and-balance check should be run on the machine as per the Bensen

Fig. 5-6. Gyrogliders are also capable of free flight. Here, towline has just been released.

manual. For greater control, a movable rudder should be installed. An airspeed indicator becomes absolutely essential at this point, as does some sort of drift indicator to help coordinate turns. If maximum-performance tow releases are desired, a shorter tow boom can be installed at the front of the ship; the standard boom is very long and, acting as a lever arm, allows the tow rope to pull the nose of the ship down at high towing angles. A shorter tow boom allows a higher maximum altitude to be reached for any given length of tow line.

The procedure for making a release is simple. First, have the driver understand that he or she is to drive faster than normal—45 mph instead of 35. When the highest practicable altitude has been reached on the tow line, the gyroglider should be dived to release tension on the tow line; then the tow release is pulled. Once free, the nose of the machine must be pointed down at about a thirty degree angle to maintain a safe glide speed of 45 mph. This is very nearly the optimum gliding speed for most gyros, and results in a descent of 500 to 700 feet per minute (depending on gross weight).

When the altitude is used up, the ship can be flared as necessary for a soft landing. The control stick should be neutralized after landing and kept neutral until the blades have decelerated considerably. A gust of wind at this point could still tip the machine over, so caution must be exercised.

Other Ideas

Gyrogliders are enormously versatile. They can be fitted with floats and towed behind a boat. A "gyroboat" can be made by fitting a rotor mast and outriggers to a small boat hull. An extra seat can be added to take friends or family members along. (The experimental Bensen B-14 gyroglider was flown with three men aboard.) And, of course, an engine can be mounted for powered free flights.

Whatever the ultimate goal, there is probably no safer, easier, or less expensive way to get started in rotorcraft than to build and fly a gyroglider.

Chapter 6
Flying the Gyrocopter

The gyrocopter is a deceptively simple machine. It amounts to little more than a keel, mast, and axle supporting a pilot, a rotor, an engine, and a rudder. Before we discuss the flying of this aircraft, let's look a bit closer at its "systems."

The tow boom is retained on the gyrocopter primarily because it offers a good location for instruments—but it can also be used to perform towed flights, engine off, for familiarization purposes. Most gyrocopter panels are understandably austere, typically containing a windspeed indicator, drift flag, altimeter, cylinder temperature gauge, and ignition switch (which in some cases is mounted on the rotor cheek plates above the pilot's head). Fuel quantity is read directly from the fuel tank rather than from a panel-mounted gauge. Usually six to ten gallons of fuel are carried, giving an average endurance of one and a half hours.

The drift flag mentioned above is a very important piece of equipment (although casual observers rarely think it is) since it is the pilot's only means of ascertaining whether or not he is flying in a coordinated fashion. A slip flag or drift flag is less expensive than a "skid ball" or inclinometer, and accomplishes the same thing. The flag indicates the direction of the oncoming wind flow relative to the direction in which the nose of the ship is pointed (Fig. 6-1).

Steering is afforded by a spring-centered, castoring nosewheel with provisions for the pilot's feet. Guiding the wheel with his feet, the pilot pushes forward on the left side to swivel the wheel to the right, or forward on the right side to steer left. This sounds unnatural at first, but it really is not much different from a toy tricycle. At any rate, direct nosewheel steering is only used at airspeeds less than ten miles per hour; otherwise, the airflow over the tail is sufficient to allow rudder steering. Braking action results from the pilot pushing with his heels on a square of plywood which bears down, Flintstone-style, on the nosewheel tire. Primitive, but it works!

Controls on a typical gyrocopter include a side-mounted, lever-type throttle (although a twist-grip, stick-mounted throttle is standard equipment on Bensen gyros), a control stick, and conventional rudder pedals which operate separately from the wholly independent nosewheel steering. The rudder is cable-actuated: push left to go left, or right to go right. The throttle is also cable-actuated and feeds power directly to the pusher propeller located about arm's length behind the pilot. The joystick acts through pushrods running up either side of the mast to physically displace the rotor head in the desired direction of movement. (For convenience, we will assume throughout this chapter that a joystick, rather than an overhead stick, is being used.)

As mentioned in the first chapter, a gyro's rotor blades are set at a fixed pitch and do not feather. Aluminum rotor blades can be assembled or disassembled from the rotor head in a matter of ten minutes using nothing but a torque wrench. Most gyro owners transport their machines on trailers, with the rotor blades individually packed in long boxes until the destination is reached, then the blades are assembled to the hub bar and the works mounted atop the ship.

Ground Operations

As with any aircraft, a flight in a gyrocopter begins with a thorough preflight inspection. One should be particularly careful to insure that the correct torque was used in putting together the rotor; that safety wire and/or cotter pins are present where they should be; that the rudder is free to move (some like to secure the rudder for road transportation) and the rudder cables are in their tracks and are not frayed; that the propeller is on tight; rotor controls are working properly; there is no excessive play in the rotor head; the slip flag and airspeed indicators are in place (these are left off for road transportation); and all seat, engine, and instrument attachments are secure. It only takes five minutes to scrutinize a gyrocopter thoroughly. Therefore, one should do this while on the ground so that there is nothing to worry about while cruising at 100 feet. (Such as: "Oh boy, did I forget to install the cotter pin on the teeter bolt?")

Naturally, be sure that all onlookers are at a safe distance before attempting to start the motor. If your copter has parking brakes, set them; if not, find good wheel chocks and use them. Wheel chocks, however, will not do the job if the engine comes alive at full throttle.

Each pilot soon develops his own unique starting ritual. For a McCulloch-powered gyro, it might go like this: Switch off (magneto grounded); pull the prop through a few times; using a squirt-can filled with high-test aviation gasoline, walk around to the rear of the ship to punch a few shots of juice into the exhaust ports of the engine; fuel line pressurized; a few priming strokes of the throttle; switch on; then pull the prop through carefully. The proper position

Fig. 6-1. Flag is most assuredly not for cosmetic value! Drift flag acts as inexpensive turn coordinator and is one of the gyro pilot's most important pieces of equipment. Thermometer-like device is airspeed indicator which is accurate in 20 to 80 mph range. For many gyrocopters, these two items are the sole "instruments" on the panel.

Fig. 6-2. Proper engine propping stance requires the pilot to straddle the axle, facing the left side of the ship. Once the engine comes to life, the pilot can stand forward of the axle, as shown here, and bring the engine to fast idle before hand-turning the rotor blades to 50 or 60 rpm.

for hand-propping a gyro is to stand facing the left side of the machine with one foot planted in front of the axle, and the other foot in back of the axle. With the left hand, grab the front of the mast, and with the right hand pull the prop down. Obviously, hand-starting any aircraft engine alone is a risky affair; it is always best to have a second person assist (Fig. 6-2).

Now, if the magneto is in good condition, and the spark plugs are not fouled or incorrectly gapped (not more than a gap of .018"), and a fuel-oil mixture is reaching the cylinders, the engine should fire within the first two pulls of the prop. Some disbelievers will maintain that no McCulloch will start with such regularity. However, many a McCulloch owner knows differently.

When the engine comes to life, keep it idling by paying close attention to the throttle. Then begin to hand-whirl the rotor blades to 50 or 60 rpm in the manner described in the last chapter (Fig. 6-3). If you can enlist the aid of a friend to do this while you buckle into the seat, so much the better. Always be sure to wear a helmet *and visor* to protect the eyes. You wouldn't think of riding a motorcycle on the freeway without eye protection; neither should you fly a gyrocopter without such protection.

As you taxi away from the pit area, you'll find that it will be necessary to ride the brakes in order to keep speed under control, even at idle thrust. Due to the nosewheel geometry, avoid braking while turning. Be very careful with throttle application when the rotor is turning at low rpm, because one good blast will send you hurtling across the tarmack with startling alacrity. At higher rotor speeds, of course, the rotor acts as an aerodynamic brake; but until rotor rpm builds to about 150, the gyrocopter is one heck of a fast three-wheel go-kart.

Getting the blades up to flight speed is the next concern. As with the gyroglider, this is done in a step-wise fashion. It bears repeating that if the blades are not turning at least 50 rpm prior to leaving the pit area, the oncoming airflow will not keep the blades turning during taxi no matter what combination of technique and black magic the pilot uses. Also, if the blades are not turning very fast there will be insufficient centrifugal force acting on the blades to keep them from putting severe stresses on the rotor head when a

Fig. 6-3. Ken Brock starts his rotor blades while holding the joystick forward and standing with one foot on the nosewheel brake. Note Brock's hard plastic seat which doubles as fuel tank.

pothole, beer can, or other irregularity is encountered on the taxiway. (I was once told by Gordon Hunt, Chief Engineer of the now defunct Avian Gyroplane project of Canada, how at one time their prototype ship lost a rotor blade as the pilot hit a rough spot on the taxiway. The rotor was not turning.) Taxiing without rotor speed is contrary to the recommendations of the Bensen manual as well as several other approved rotorcraft manuals.

The initial taxiing should be done at less than ten mph *airspeed* so as to allow the rotor blades to accelerate without flapping against the teeter stop. If at any time before takeoff a two-per-rev shake in the control stick is noticed, power must be reduced and the joystick brought forward at once. The taxi or takeoff roll may be resumed when the stick can be brought fully back without any sign of vibration.

After the rotor has reached 100 rpm or so (the pilot will have to use his own judgment on this since gyrocopters lack rotor tachometers), the speed can be increased to 15 mph. In the 100 to 200 rpm range, the rotor still is not producing much drag, so a relatively minor increase of power can result in a sprightly increase in ground speed. Throttle should be used judiciously.

After approximately thirty seconds at 15 mph airspeed, the rotor will reach a plateau around 200 rpm. For the first time, the individual rotor blades will be hard to see, and various aural cues will tell the pilot that the machine is beginning to come alive. When this point is reached, the pilot should switch from nosewheel steering to the use of rudder pedals. At the new rpm, the rotor is beginning to produce significant drag, and because of this a fair amount of throttle can be applied without causing a new world land speed record to be set.

Continuing the takeoff roll at 20 mph, with the stick all the way back, the rotor is allowed to accelerate further. After a few seconds, a small nudge can be given to the throttle; when the rotor "catches up," so to speak, another nudge can be given to the throttle. Soon, the entire machine will without warning rock backward onto the tail wheel; the rotor is ready to fly. Now is when the action really begins.

Up, Up, and Away

The best thing to do now is slowly (but not terribly slowly) advance the throttle until the engine is delivering peak power. Simultaneously, the stick must be brought forward to bring the nosewheel back down. Ideally, the takeoff roll should be completed with neither nosewheel nor tailwheel touching the ground. This requires practice, naturally. If the craft is then maintained in the "balanced" position—main wheels only on the ground—then at about 35 mph the machine will lift off and the pilot will be on his way.

It's very important that the machine break ground in a level attitude—that is, the tail wheel should not be the last wheel to leave the runway. If full power is applied with the joystick full aft, the gyrocopter will part company with the runway unexpectedly at around 25 mph at an extreme angle of attack, with the rotor blades clearing the ground by mere inches. Flying in a mush, the ship will probably contact the ground as unexpectedly as it left it; there will be no climb performance. Conversely, if too much forward stick pressure is used on the takeoff roll, it is likely that the gyro will not lift off until 50 or 60 mph, and then it will come off nosewheel last. This situation is known as wheelbarrowing and is risky either in gyrocopters or airplanes.

Just at the instant of liftoff, the machine may display a momentary banking tendency in one direction or the other. This should be anticipated for and correction made without overcontrolling. Once free of the ground, the pilot should make an immediate check of his drift indicator. Rudder should be applied as necessary to keep the flag pointing right at the pilot. Coordinated flight is imperative when operating close to the ground.

The acceleration experienced directly after becoming airborne is nothing short of stupefying and will cause the inexperienced gyrocopter pilot to want to "climb on out" to a higher altitude at once. Ground effect will contribute to the machine's tendency (aided by the pilot) to want to climb. It would be unwise, however, to climb higher than five or six feet until a speed of 50 or 60 mph registers on the airspeed indicator. Without this extra speed, safe recovery from a sudden power loss would be made difficult. To put it another way, at least 50 mph is needed in order for a flare to be executed, and because of this, there is no way to make a soft landing if the pilot is flying at 40 mph when the engine malfunctions. A prudent practice is never to climb higher than five feet without at least 50 mph of indicated airspeed.

Air Work

Once airborne, the joystick-equipped gyrocopter handles in much the same way as any light fixed-wing aircraft, except that the controls are responsive throughout the speed range from Vne (90 mph) down to zero mph. Because rotor rmp is self-governing, a gyrocopter—unlike a helicopter—need not carry a rotor tachometer. Once airborne, there is very little a pilot can do about the gyro's rotor speed.

If the gyroglider was mastered before undertaking powered flight, the stick should feel very comfortable. The new items, throttle and rudder, must be operated in a coordinated fashion and will take some getting used to for the novice. For that reason, beginners should start out making low and high speed tail runs and many short, one or two foot high hops off the ground before attempting to leave ground effect. An intelligent pilot would no sooner take a gyrocopter around the traffic pattern on his first flight than he would attempt to check himself out in a Formula One racer after an hour's dual in a Cessna 150.

A turn to the left requires only a nudge of the stick to the left, with some back pressure if the turn is more than a few degrees in bank. Rudder should be applied only as necessary to center the drift flag; power should be applied to maintain altitude. Opposite stick and rudder will stop the turn. That's it.

Probably an inch of stick deflection in any direction will accomplish most maneuvers. This is not to say that the gyrocopter is "touchy"—far from it. Most gyrocopters will fly hands-off, something that almost no other rotarywing aircraft will do.

Because the rotor turns at a more or less constant rpm no matter what the craft's actual speed, control is excellent at all times. Proof of this comes when one tries to "stall" a gyro. Power can be left on or off; if the pilot brings the stick back slowly, letting airspeed gradually bleed off, all that happens is that the copter goes from cruise to slow forward flight to a modest vertical descent of 1,000 feet per minute. That's 17 feet per second, or about the same rate as a parachute. To fly out of the maneuver, simply apply power and dive to gain airspeed. If no power is applied, a glide speed of 45 mph yields a tame 700 ft./min. rate of descent.

The Power Curve

Both the best glide speed and best rate of climb speed for gyrocopters happen to fall around 45 mph. The reason for this is that level-flight drag is at a minimum at this speed; below or above 45 mph, drag skyrockets. Thus, the lift over drag ratio is optimum at this airspeed and, because the power required to maintain level flight is proportional to drag, the greatest usable power reserve exists at this airspeed.

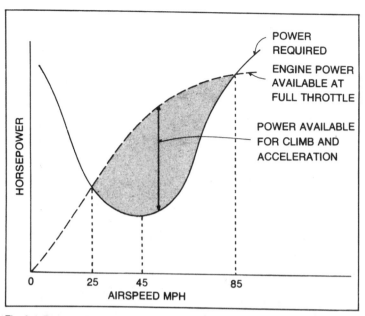

Fig. 6-4. Power-required and power-available curves for an average gyrocopter. Power available is plotted as a function of propeller efficiency. See text for discussion.

These relationships are shown by the so-called *power curves* for the gyrocopter. This is nothing more than a graph which plots power (or thrust or percent throttle) vertically and airspeed horizontally; the two curves shown on it are the "power required" and "power available" curves (Fig. 6-4). The first curve depicts the relationship between airspeed, and the power needed to maintain level flight at that airspeed. As we've already hinted, this curve is bathtub-shaped, reaching bottom at 45 mph. The second curve, as its name indicates, shows the maximum power available from the engine at any airspeed. (This curve would be a horizontal line if propeller efficiency, which varies with airspeed, were not taken into account.)

Close inspection of this graph will reveal several important facts about gyrocopter performance. One is that, to go faster than 45 mph in level flight requires a power increase; but to go *slower* than 45 mph in level flight *also requires a power increase.* Secondly, it will be seen that the "power required" curve intersects the "power available" curve at around 25 mph. This means that 25 mph is the minimum level flight speed—the speed at which full throttle is needed in order to maintain altitude. Below this speed, only descending flight can occur. The two curves also cross again in the high-speed region of the graph, the point where they cross indicated the maximum speed of the aircraft.

The power curve graph is often divided in half at the 45 mph mark, the portion dealing with airspeeds over 45 mph being called the "front side" and the portion below 45 mph being named the "back side" of the power curve. The "back side" is important to safety considerations, because this is the region in which more and more power is needed to fly at lower and lower speeds, a seemingly contradictory situation (Fig. 6-5). Many gyrocopter accidents have occurred directly as a result of pilot ignorance with regard to this area of aircraft performance. Because he is flying a "stall-proof" machine, a new gyrocopter pilot may assume that it's perfectly safe to buzz along at telephone-pole height with only 35 or 40 mph showing on the airspeed indicator. Tragedy occurs when this pilot's engine starts to run rough (spark plug fouling is common), or when he allows airspeed to decay out of carelessness, or when an improperly coordinated turn is attempted.

The lesson is simple: flying on the back side of the power curve should be attempted only at high altitude. (For speeds of less than 35 mph, this means at least 500 feet.) Flight near the ground should always be conducted with sufficient airspeed to allow a safe landing

Fig. 6-5. Ken Brock demonstrates the "back of the power curve" flying; see the dust washing behind the prop in this very high drag manuever.

Fig. 6-6. A gyroplane can be landed in a very small space. Here Ken Brock lands on the dock in Long Beach near the Queen Mary and Hughes Spruce Goose.

in the event of engine malfunction. *Always maintain at least 50 mph when flying close to the ground.*

Landing

Landing a gyrocopter is not terribly different from landing a Cessna 150 except that the rollout will be about 400 feet shorter (Fig. 6-6).

Some power should be left on for the approach, unless the pilot is experienced. An approach speed of 50 mph is advisable. Speeds slightly less than this can be used, but not much less, for reasons described on previous page. Throughout the approach, glide slope should be adjusted with the power only and airspeed with the control stick only.

When the gyro passes through about twenty feet altitude, the rate of descent will slow due to ground effect. The approach angle will actually flatten out, if the pilot lets it, and airspeed will start to decay. The pilot should be on guard for this and anticipate the entry of ground effect by reducing throttle at around twenty feet altitude, keeping glide slope and airspeed constant all the way to the ground. The ground cushion will build up as the craft gets closer and closer to touchdown; hence, and throttle can be retarded continuously.

Several feet from the ground, the flare can begin. If any throttle remains, it should be taken off. During the flare, the machine is subjected to a slight extra load factor (G-loading) which will cause the rotor to spin faster, creating additional lift and making the ship want to float at the exact moment that the pilot wishes to be touching down. (An excess of airspeed upon entering ground effect also leads to floating.) While skimming along one foot or so above the ground, the controls will seem sensitive, making it easy for the pilot to balloon five or ten feet into the air. The pilot should be alert to this (Fig. 6-7).

After a few seconds, any excess speed or lift will dissipate and it will be time to land. By "holding it off" as long as possible with the stick, it's possible to decelerate very quickly to a very low speed and roll out in only ten feet or so. The precise touchdown speed is not important so long as the main wheels touch first and the machine does not touch down in a crabbed attitude.

Two common difficulties are, landing too soon, and landing too high and dropping in. Landing too soon means forcing the ship on the runway with an excess of airspeed and rotor speed—that is, not holding the ship off long enough with the stick. After a longer-than-normal landing roll, what will happen is that a few seconds after touching down the entire craft will suddenly rock back onto the tailwheel. When rotor rpm has dissipated, the ship will then come back down on the nosewheel. (A harmless idiosyncracy, but it can be startling.) Dropping in is the result of flaring too high off the ground and landing literally in midair. All the throttle in the world

Fig. 6-7. Correct altitude for landing is shown in this picture. Pilot is holding the machine mere inches off the ground simultaneously retarding throttle completely. Rollout will be approximately ten feet.

won't prevent the hard bounce that follows. Hard landings can cause structural deformations, and are not good for blood pressure either. Remember, a free fall from six inches is equivalent to hitting the ground in a 340-foot-per-minute descent.

Post-Flight

The rotor will decelerate quickly after landing, but never simply let the control stick go where it will; a gust of wind can sometimes catch the rotor just right, particularly if the machine is turning to taxi back, to tip the gyro over. Never let your guard down until the engine is stopped and the rotor secured.

Some pilots stop their engines by turning off the fuel; others like to turn off the ignition. After the engine is off, the carburetor opening should be covered and the blades tied with a cord to the tow boom so they can't move.

So now you have a rough idea of what gyrocopter flight involves. In reality, it is more complicated and more subtle in many ways than has been represented here. However, gyrocopter flying is a skill that, like any other skill, can be learned. I know of no better, easier way for an amateur to obtain an education in rotarywing flight than to build and fly a gyrocopter.

Chapter 7
Flying the Helicopter

As one manufacturer's brochure states, "The helicopter is capable of landing and taking off in a spot just large enough to swing its rotor blades." This is something a gyrocopter just won't do, and it's also a capability that more and more builders have come to seek, guided along their way by libido-enriching color ads and daydreams of Sunday afternoon picnics at lake-front landing pads.

To some people—those with $20,000 to spend on dream machines—the noise, low payload, and long takeoffs of gyrocopters are insufferable handicaps compared with the quiet and comfort of a brightly colored two-man helicopter. As a result, homebuilt helicopters are now a million dollar a year business attracting a good number of middle-class Americans into its folds.

Although the performance offered by a helicopter is appealing, few people fully realize what the piloting of a helicopter entails. Most pilots simply shrug when they are told that learning to fly a homebuilt helicopter is different from any other learning experience they're likely to have encountered, or when experts recommend several hundred dollars worth the dual instruction in a Hughes, Enstrom, or Bell prior to even sitting down in a homebuilt helo.

In truth, a helicopter is very much different to fly than any other aircraft. More concentration, more coordination, and more stamina are required in helicopter flight. Pilots speak kindly however, when they label the helicopter "a pilot's machine."

Controls

Because the helicopter's rotor blades are free to feather and flap, the controls of a homebuilt copter are different from those of a gyro. They are not, however, different from those of a larger, commercial helicopter (Figs. 7-1, 7-2).

In the pilot's lap is an implement that looks something like a bowed joystick. This is the *cyclic stick control*. The word cyclic refers to the fact that displacement of this control is a given direction causes the rotor blades to vary in pitch in a cyclic fashion as they travel around the rotor disc, ultimately causing aerodynamic forces to incline the tip path plane in the given direction. In a gyrocopter, moving the stick physically tilts the rotor head (and the axis of rotation of the rotor) in the desired direction. In a helicopter, the rotational axis of the rotor lies along the rotor shaft and never changes; the blades move relative to the shaft.

Along the left side of the pilot's seat is still another stick. This one is called the *collective pitch control*. By raising or lowering it, one simultaneously changes the angle of incidence of all the rotor blades (however many there are) an equal amount at once. That is, the blades are feathered collectively. This control is used to alter altitude; raising it increases the "bite" of the rotor blades and causes the machine to rise.

At the end of the collective is a twist-grip throttle. With his left hand, the pilot twists inward or outward to close or open throttle, thus altering engine rpm.

Directional, or yaw, control is afforded by foot pedals which act (via cables) to increase or decrease the pitch of the tail rotor blades (Fig. 7-3). These pedals are similar in function to the rudder pedals of an airplane, but in helicopter jargonese are properly referred to as *anti-torque control pedals* or *tail rotor pedals*. Or simply "pedals."

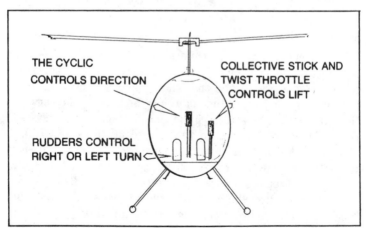

THE CYCLIC
CONTROLS DIRECTION

COLLECTIVE STICK AND
TWIST THROTTLE
CONTROLS LIFT

RUDDERS CONTROL
RIGHT OR LEFT TURN

Fig. 7-1. Helicopter basic flight controls.

Fig. 7-2. Controls of a homebuilt helicopter include foot pedals, cyclic control in center, and collective with twist-grip throttle (visible in lower part of picture). Instrument panel features engine and rotor tachs, airspeed indicator, time-elapsed meter, engine temp. gauge.

Already we can see that the helicopter pilot has no spare hands for juggling maps, microphones, or Thermos bottles. He literally has his hands full. Just how full, we'll soon see.

The Hover

Learning to hover has been likened to trying to stand on a beach ball in the deep end of a swimming pool. Control lag, engine and rotor rpm constraints, and other problems contribute to the beginner's having a hard time of it. Yet the hover is the very first thing that must be mastered if the amateur builder-pilot hopes to realize his most cherished rotarywing dreams (Figs. 7-4, 7-5).

RotorWay, Inc., has long recommended the use of a six-inch tether for early hover practice. Six inches may not sound like much, but a lot can happen in this paltry altitude allotment. Before beginning hover practice, the builder should have spent several hours breaking in the engine, practicing rpm control during ground run-ups, and checking out the aircraft for any unusual vibrations.

Fig. 7-3. The anti-torque end of a helicopter. Tail rotor on this Scorpion is driven by belts; collective pitch of the tail rotor blades is varied by foot pedals in the cockpit. Note horizontal stabilizer on tail boom.

RotorWay has a checklist of over a hundred items demanding inspection before the first test hop.

Why not go out to the airport, spend two hours with an instructor in a Hughes 300, then after learning how to hover the Hughes, come home and start flying the homebuilt *sans* tether? Well, al-

Fig. 7-4. Learning to hover a helicopter requires concentrated effort. But like riding a bike, once you know how, it's easy.

Fig. 7-5. Hovering is almost as much fun to watch as to do! Spectators, however, should be kept well clear at all times.

though the principles involved in hovering a homebuilt and a Hughes are the same, still there are subtle differences between the two that would never allow a person to step right from one into the other. The Scorpion's rotor, for instance, turns opposite to the Hughes' rotor, meaning that torque control will be reversed. Also, the Scorpion is lighter than the Hughes and has a faster-turning rotor, factors contributing to the Scorpion having a different cyclic response than the Hughes. Similarly, throttle reaction time and the range of collective stick control will be different for the two helicopters. In short, control coordination in the two copters is different. Being able to fly one is no assurance of being able to fly the other.

Because of this, do not let anyone (no matter what their credentials) try to hover your homebuilt without a tether. More than one homebuilt helicopter has been destroyed after a hot-shot "helicopter pilot" lost control in a hover.

What makes hovering a helicopter so unique? Let's look at what's involved. The object is to feed *just enough* power to the rotor to overcome the pull of gravity, and at the same time stay over one spot on the ground. To generate just the right amount of lift requires that the rotor turn at the right rpm, with the rotor blades set at just the right pitch setting using the collective.

We therefore begin by spinning the rotor up to speed with the collective in the full down position. As the throttle is smoothly opened, the blades will accelerate slowly until they reach the flight-rpm range shown by a green arc on the rotor tachometer. Usually, this range encompasses a total spread of 50 or 75 rpm; it's up to the pilot to keep the rotor in this range at all times. If the rpm is allowed to decay, the rotor blades may cone excessively and tail rotor control will be lost, since the tail rotor is driven off of the main rotor and must have adequate rpm to ensure directional control. If rpm is allowed to get too high, the rotor head and blade retention straps could be overstressed, reducing rotor life. Likewise, engine rpm must be kept within a narrow range not only for maximum efficiency of the motor itself, but to keep rotor rpm from going every which way.

Once the engine and rotor are turning at their proper rpm it is advisable, prior to each takeoff, to chop the throttle and see that as the engine rpm plunges precipitously, the rotor continues to freewheel. This is called "splitting the needles"—the tach needles should diverge, not stay together. The freewheeling clutch which allows the rotor to turn independently of engine rpm is a necessary safety feature if an autorotation landing is to be possible following engine seizure.

With engine and rotor rpm each returned to their proper ranges, and with the cyclic neutralized or positioned slightly into the wind, the takeoff can proceed. Assuming, for convenience, that the helicopter in question is a Scorpion, we can expect the airframe to want to turn counterclockwise when power is applied to the clockwise-turning (looking from above) rotor. Hence, right pedal will have to be applied as power is increased. The more power, the more torque and the more right pedal. Before raising the collective, a good deal of right pedal will be applied.

When raising the collective rotor drag increases due to the new, higher pitch setting of the rotor blades. This extra drag will tend to slow the rotor down unless a corrective amount of power is added. (Likewise, upon lowering the collective, the blades will tend to overspeed unless power is subtracted.) Happily, most conventional helicopters have a linkage coupling the collective arm with the throttle so as to automatically feed in more throttle as the collective is raised; such a linkage is called *correlation*. The Scorpion employs correlation between its collective and throttle. Nonetheless, the pilot must make small throttle adjustments in hover to keep rpm where it should be.

The liftoff is made by raising the collective slowly and applying right pedal as necessary, until the machine is perceptively buoyant. As the skids lighten, the pilot can sense whether or not he needs to add more right pedal, reposition the cyclic, etc. Throttle adjustments, as always, should be made by way of a "slow squeeze." It is often said that if a helicopter pilot's control movements are visible to an observer, then he is not flying properly. One should learn to "think" more power, or more left cyclic, rather than abruptly moving these controls.

At last, upon raising the collective a final inch or so, the copter will levitate. In hover, the pilot will notice that the cyclic, aside from having no "feel" or aerodynamic feedback, does not respond in the same way as an airplane's joystick: there is a definite control lag, such that the copter will move in response to short jabs of the cyclic only after a certain time period has elapsed. The lack of positive "feel" to the cyclic and its delayed reaction time usually contribute to overcontrolling on the part of beginners. The new pilot will be slow to react to pitch and roll perturbations, since his attention is being distracted to a large degree by the other controls. This can lead to things getting out of hand rather quickly. Clearly, the cyclic demands a fair amount of attention during the hover—you can forget about hands-off flight.

Because of small wind gusts, engine power variations, and airflow disturbances, it will be virtually impossible to maintain a constant altitude without some minor adjustments of collective. Moreover, this means pedal pressures will need to be altered, for even a slight movement of the collective engenders a large change in torque. Downward movement of the collective must be coordinated with left pedal pressure; upward movement, by right pedal pressure.

Inevitably, small wind gusts or power changes will also cause the nose to drift either to the right or to the left. Immediate corrective action should be taken. One will note, however, that depression of the right pedal will cause the tail rotor to work harder, drawing more power from the engine. As a result, the ship will begin to settle and rpm tapers off unless more throttle and collective are applied as needed. Conversely, a lessening of right pedal pressure will mean that the tail rotor is working less hard against torque and the helicopter may begin to rise slightly.

Common mistakes made by learners are: letting rotor or engine rpm go beyond their limits; overcontrolling the cyclic or collective; reacting too late to disturbances of heading, position over ground, or altitude. All of these errors are interrelated, each compounding the other. Perhaps it can now be appreciated why beginners emerge from their first hovering attempt so worn out.

Air Taxiing

"Air taxi maneuvers" are the next category of new skills to be practiced by the novitiate once the tether ropes have been dropped.

Air taxiing refers to operations performed by a helicopter within several feet of the ground and at speeds between usually 5 and 10 mph. Air taxiing is not only a way to get around on a busy airport, but offers excellent coordination exercises for the learner.

To this point, all hovers will have been practiced faced squarely into the wind. However, air taxi maneuvers require that the pilot know how to hover while facing downwind as well as crosswind. An exception is that if the wind speed exceeds ten knots, no turns or hovers should be made at more than ninety degrees to the wind line. Directional control can be lost when hovering in a strong quartering crosswind.

Forward air taxiing should be practiced, and sideways flight and backing up as well. Then, precision turns of 90, 180, and 360 degrees should be practiced over a point on the ground, in both directions. These maneuvers will fine-tune the new pilot's pedal and throttle coordination.

Technique can be further improved through the practice of so-called "square patterns." This involves hovering the ship around the perimeter of a 20-foot square on the ground, with the nose of the ship always pointing toward the inside of the square. The maneuver can be performed also with the tail of the ship always pointing toward the square. Several other interesting variations are possible (Fig. 7-6).

Translation

Translation—that is, the transition to forward flight—can occur very quickly in a small, light helicopter. New sensations tend to confuse the pilot and new coordinations must be learned. There-

Fig. 7-6. Backwards flight will be practiced in air taxi phase of training.

Fig. 7-7. Translational flight should not be attempted until the pilot has mastered hovering and air taxi maneuvers, as new sensations encountered by the pilot may cause him to become disoriented.

fore, the new pilot must approach translational flight slowly and with due caution.

Translation is initiated simply by applying forward pressure to the cyclic from a normal hover, simultaneously increasing collective pitch somewhat. (The pilot will already be using more than half the available collective travel just to maintain a hover. On a hot day or at high gross weights, the full amount of available collective may be needed to break ground.) Right pedal pressure should be applied as needed to keep a straight track across the ground.

As speed is acquired, the ship will begin to feel different. *Translational lift* can be felt at around 15 mph. Between the speeds of 15 and 40 mph, the rush of air meeting the top of the rotor acts to improve the rotor's efficiency and the helicopter will actually seem to acquire more lift, as if by magic. This lift is very real, and when it is encountered the pilot will find that less collective pitch and pedal pressure are needed to continue flight in a given attitude (Figs. 7-7, 7-8).

When a forward speed of 40 or 50 mph is attained, a sustained climbout may begin. To keep this airspeed, the *cyclic* should be repositioned fore or aft as required. To increase or decrease the rate of climb, the collective should be moved.

Cruise

To level out, the cyclic can be nudged forward a bit, then the collective lowered slightly. Cruise speed will be in the neighborhood of 70 mph, depending upon the exact power setting used. At this forward speed, weathervaning helps keep the tail straight back behind the copter and so less attention to the pedals will be needed. Any noticeable displacment of the collective, however, may necessitate some use of pedals to keep a straight heading.

Turns are accomplished primarily through cyclic action; little or no pedal pressure need be applied, as the tail will continue to weathervane behind the aircraft. If the turn is at all steep, forward cyclic pressure may be required to maintain airspeed, while more collective may be needed to maintain altitude. Opposite cyclic will terminate the turn.

High-speed flight should be approached with caution. If the helicopter is not properly trimmed or stabilized about the pitch axis, particularly if the center of gravity is out of limits, control could be lost. If any oscillations or vibrations are felt at high speeds, flight should be confined to normal cruise operations until the nature of the vibration has been determined.

Descents and Autorotations

Normal descents are accomplished by lowering the collective partway, using left rudder as necessary to maintain heading, and adjusting the airspeed to around 50 mph with the cyclic.

Arresting the descent is a matter of bringing the cyclic back to slow the copter down and initially flatten the glide. Eventually, collective must be cranked in to maintain altitude. Naturally, throughout these control manipulations the pilot, as always, will be paying attention to the two tachometers, adding engine or rotor rpm as needed and coordinating with rudder pedal as required (Figs. 7-9, 7-10).

It's natural to ask: What happens if the engine quits? The answer is, the instant the engine quits, the helicopter becomes a gyroglider. If a sudden silence should occur in flight, the pilot's

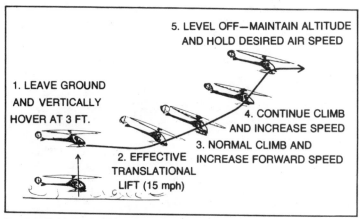

5. LEVEL OFF—MAINTAIN ALTITUDE AND HOLD DESIRED AIR SPEED

1. LEAVE GROUND AND VERTICALLY HOVER AT 3 FT.

4. CONTINUE CLIMB AND INCREASE SPEED

3. NORMAL CLIMB AND INCREASE FORWARD SPEED

2. EFFECTIVE TRANSLATIONAL LIFT (15 mph)

Fig. 7-8. Takeoff, standard procedure.

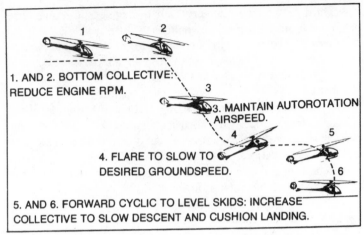

1. AND 2. BOTTOM COLLECTIVE: REDUCE ENGINE RPM.

3. MAINTAIN AUTOROTATION AIRSPEED.

4. FLARE TO SLOW TO DESIRED GROUNDSPEED.

5. AND 6. FORWARD CYCLIC TO LEVEL SKIDS: INCREASE COLLECTIVE TO SLOW DESCENT AND CUSHION LANDING.

Fig. 7-9. A standard helicopter landing can be made as long as there is space to swing the blades.

instinctive reaction should be to lower the collective immediately. (If he fails to do this, the rotor will decelerate dangerously.) This will put the helicopter in an autorotational descent. The cyclic should be repositioned to give an airspeed indication of around 50

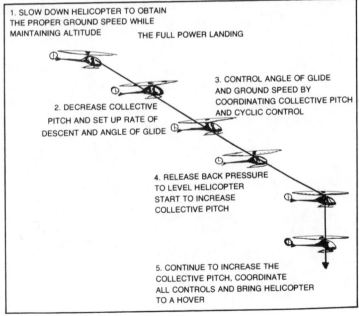

1. SLOW DOWN HELICOPTER TO OBTAIN THE PROPER GROUND SPEED WHILE MAINTAINING ALTITUDE

THE FULL POWER LANDING

2. DECREASE COLLECTIVE PITCH AND SET UP RATE OF DESCENT AND ANGLE OF GLIDE

3. CONTROL ANGLE OF GLIDE AND GROUND SPEED BY COORDINATING COLLECTIVE PITCH AND CYCLIC CONTROL

4. RELEASE BACK PRESSURE TO LEVEL HELICOPTER START TO INCREASE COLLECTIVE PITCH

5. CONTINUE TO INCREASE THE COLLECTIVE PITCH, COORDINATE ALL CONTROLS AND BRING HELICOPTER TO A HOVER

Fig. 7-10. The hovering approach landing.

mph. This will minimize the rate of descent—which, depending on the disc loading and the air density, could range from 800 to 2,000 feet per minute—and allow for a safe flare-out to be executed before touching down (Figs. 7-11, 7-12).

Somewhere between 50 and 100 feet altitude, the cyclic can be brought back to flatten the glide and dissipate airspeed. Some forward cyclic may have to be used at the last moment to keep the tail from digging in; in the very last seconds before reaching the ground, collective stick should be used to soften the impact. If proper technique has been throughout, a "full-on" autorotation landing can be made without damaging either the ship or its occupants.

The last "if" is a big one: in order for proficiency to be maintained, autorotations to a power-recovery landing should be practiced by the experienced pilot on a regular basis. No autorotations, however, should be attempted by untrained novices, nor should full-on (zero power all the way) landings be practiced. Many

Fig. 7-11. A helicopter can "glide" if a power failure occurs. When autorotations are practiced, recovery should begin at about 50 feet altitude as shown here.

Fig. 7-12. As the ground is approached, collective is used at the end of autorotation to cushion landing. Stored energy in the blades will keep the rotor turning for a few seconds after applying collective—the more massive the blades, the longer they will continue to turn, without power, when collective has been applied.

thousands of hours of military and commercial helicopter operations have shown that the continual practice of zero-power autorotation landings constitutes a greater hazard to personnel and equipment than does the practice of power-recovery autorotations.

In case the reader has gotten the impression that helicopter autorotations are risky and frightful, let me just say that I don't know any helicopter pilot who would choose to dead-stick an airplane from 10,000 feet rather than be forced to make an autorotation from 1,000 feet in a helicopter. For, as was said at the beginning of this chapter, a helicopter can be landed or taken off from a spot just big enough to swing its blades; not so an airplane that quits flying at less than 60 mph.

Gray Areas

The gray areas of a helicopter's performance envelope are not at all obvious, in most instances, and thus can be wandered into quite unwittingly by a beginner. Before leaving the topic of helicopter flight, then, perhaps we should enumerate some of these Twilight Zones and their implications for safety.

We have mentioned briefly that turns of more than 90 degrees from the wind line should be avoided while hovering in a strong wind. This is primarily because the tail rotor is incapable of putting out sufficient thrust to counteract rapidly enough the tendency of the wind to swing the tail around. If a 180 degree turn is attempted from an upwind to a downwind facing position, the wind can blow the tail rotor back around at the completion of the maneuver, resulting in loss of directional control. The effects of crosswinds on tail rotor effectiveness are such as to make engine rpm control difficult, particularly when the direction of the wind is varied by turning. These suggestions may sound rather benign on paper, but rest assured many a student has "lost it" when attempting to air taxi in a stiff breeze.

High speed flight can be another so-called gray area, especially for homebuilt machines that might harbor hidden vibrational modes or instability patterns peculiar to that one individual machine. It should be noted that helicopters, contrary to other forms of aircraft, lack dynamic stability in cruise and will not necessarily return to level flight following a sudden alteration of the flight path. Neutral stability is often achievable using a properly placed horizontal fin on the tail boom. However, machines with unusual cabin enclosures or improper C. G. placement can be and often are unstable at high speeds regardless of fin design. Always follow the manufacturer's recommendations with regard to determining Vne (never-exceed velocity) for any homebuilt.

Another precautionary flight zone is represented by hovering out of ground effect (H.O.G.E.) Hovering in ground effect, which is to say within one rotor diameter of the ground, requires a great deal of power even though an air "cushion" has built up underneath the machine. Hovering in midair well clear of the ground is a feat calling for horsepower which may or may not be available. This is a perfect setup for what is known as "settling in your own downwash." The latter phenomenon occurs when the copter, for reasons either of insufficient power or misjudgment of altitude, enters a very slow descent, only to enter a flight mode in which rotor rpm is lost and engine power insufficient to regain rotor speed. What happens is that the blades, operating at a high pitch setting, fly into their own descending drag eddies, whereupon both lift and rotor rpm are eroded. The only cure is to enter translational flight at once, and regain rotor rpm even if it means entering autorotation. Since recovery usually requires a significant altitude trade-off, "settling" should be avoided at all costs while operating at heights of only one or two hundred feet. In general, it is a good idea to avoid hovering out of ground effect except when absolutely necessary.

So much for gray areas. All aircraft have their cautionary flight regimes, and helicopters are no exception. We'll have more to say about hazards of helicopter flight in the next chapter.

Chapter 8
A Word about Safety

Motorcyclists are victims of a peculiar kind of prejudice: most non-motorcycle owners think that motorcycles are inherently dangerous while, of course, cyclists by and large do not share that point of view. A similar situation prevails in the homebuilt rotorcraft arena. A large segment of the non-rotorcraft-oriented aviation public believes small gyrocopters and helicopters are a good deal more dangerous than motorcycles; but the pilots of these machines know better.

To be sure, accidents do happen; sometimes tragic ones. Between April 20, 1964, and August 13, 1967, for example, 39 accidents involving gyrocopters were recorded by the National Transportation Safety Board. But contrary to hangar mythology, the majority of these accidents was due not to circumstances beyond the pilot's control, but circumstances fully within the pilot's control. Of the 39 accidents, 30 were directly attributable to gross pilot error. Among the pilots involved, the average time-in-type was 7.6 hours. Amazingly, 16 pilots had less than two hours total time-in-type. Of the accidents involving mechancial failure—mostly engine failures—pilot indiscretion was at least indirectly to blame in many of the mishaps. Significantly, none of the mechanical failures involved Bensen-made components. (To this day, according to Bensen Aircraft Corporation, "there has never been an accident resulting from in-flight structural failure of any parts manufactured by Bensen.")

Many probable causes given for the accidents are identical to those frequently assigned fixed-wing accidents: loss of airspeed on final approach, fuel starvation, downwind turn low to the ground, improper operation of controls in crosswind, collision with power lines, etc. Nonetheless, it would be misleading to suggest that there are no "accident types" that are peculiar to homebuilt rotorcraft; there are. These accident types and the reasons for them are the subject of this chapter.

Ground-Proximity Accidents

Much of a small gyrocopter's (or helicopter's) normal flight operation occurs near the ground. Perhaps surprisingly, most pilots of homebuilt rotorcraft feel more comfortable at a 100 foot cruising altitude than at 1,000 feet. The slow cruise speed of rotarywing homebuilts makes it seem as if one is not making any progress over the ground when flying high; also, the long time it takes to climb to and descend from altitudes more than several telephone poles high contributes to the reluctance of pilots to abandon the use of low cruising altitudes. Hence, most flying is done at near-ground level. The result is that certain types of accidents are more frequent among amateur-built slingwings than might otherwise be the case. For instance, collision with unseen wires is a somewhat frequent event, as one might expect.

More insidiously, gyrocopters are prone to premature ground contact when operated "on the back side of the power curve." Pilots sometimes forget that although a gyrocopter has no "stall speed," continued flight below a certain airspeed (about 25 mph for a 90-hp gyro) inevitably leads to a loss of altitude, *regardless* of the amount of power used. Although this matter was discussed in Chapter 6, it bears repeating that an average 90-hp gyrocopter will maintain altitude, with full throttle, at 25 mph and no less. If maximum power is not available, such as is the case on a hot day or at high altitudes above sea level (or when spark plug fouling occurs), the minimum level flight speed may be closer to 35 or even 40 mph. Anytime the pilot lets his airspeed go lower than this minimum level flight speed, a descent begins which cannot be arrested by power. Recovery is only possible at the expense of altitude—hundreds of feet of altitude.

Another "ground proximity" type of accident which is frequent among homebuilt rotorcraft is the unsuccessful downwind turn; more about this in the next chapter.

The Height-Velocity Envelope

No mention is usually made of the "front" or "back" side of a helicopter's power-required curve, for the obvious reason that the power required is always less than the power available no matter what the airspeed. Nonetheless, helicopters are subject to their own particular *caveats* when operating close to the ground.

A sudden power failure in a small helicopter cruising at 60 mph at an altitude of 100 feet over clear ground poses no immediate threat to one's life expectancy; in fact, this scenario could hardly be improved upon where engine failure is concerned. A flame-out at 25 mph at the same altitude would be considerably less rosy. Why? Because to make a safe zero-zero (that is, zero altitude and zero airspeed reached simultaneously) landing after an emergency autorotation, an approach speed higher than 25 mph must be used; yet, sufficient airspeed cannot be obtained in only 100 feet of altitude loss. To put it plainly, there will be no flare-out to speak of if 50 mph cannot be attained during the descent. The situation would be even worse if the engine were to seize up while hovering at zero airspeed at 100 feet altitude.

These harsh realities are made clear in what is called a *height-velocity chart* (Fig. 8-1). Most manufacturers include a height-velocity chart in the aircraft manual. The height-velocity diagram shows altitude along the vertical axis and airspeed along the horizontal. The curves shown on this graph were obtained by plotting pairs of numbers representing the altitude loss required to achieve a safe zero-zero landing following engine failure at a given airspeed. An engine malfunction, for instance, occurring in cruise at 40 mph might necessitate a 60-foot downhill run to achieve 50 mph and thus a safe flare-out speed for landing. At 30 mph, perhaps 175 feet may be needed to accelerate to a safe speed, flare, and land. At 20 mph, perhaps 260 feet are needed. And so on, until reaching zero mph, at which point the greatest altitude loss is required in order to make a safe power-off landing. When these data points—obtained by flight trials—are plotted, one gets a typical height-velocity curve bounding an area of unsafe flight. Any flight conducted in the shaded envelope(s) is done at the pilot's risk and with full knowledge of the possible consequences should an engine failure occur.

Engine failure, nonetheless, is not the full story. For it sometimes happens that at slow airspeeds while descending the helicopter begins to fly in its own downwash. This phenomenon is called "settling" and was discussed in the last chapter—as with engine failure, a substantial altitude loss can be required for safe recovery.

And so for *this* reason, as well as for reasons of possible engine malfunction, no flight should be conducted within the shaded portions of a helicopter's height-velocity chart.

Zero-G Maneuvers

Most aircraft can withstand brief exposure to negative load factors (G-loadings of less than zero). Even multiengine airplanes placarded against negative-G maneuvers will not undergo structural damage given momentary exposure to weightlessness. The same cannot be said of homebuilt rotorcraft.

Gyrocopters in particular are very sensitive to zero-G flight, let alone negative-G flight. This is because rotor rpm is influenced by G-loading in such a way that the rotor turns faster at higher load factors, and slows down when no load is applied. If load factor is low

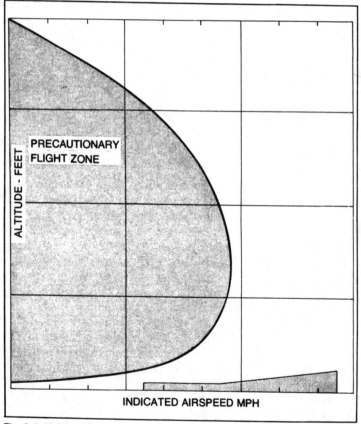

Fig. 8-1. Height-velocity curve.

enough, the rotor of a gyrocopter can decelerate irreversibly, leading to disaster.

A typical scenario is as follows. An inexperienced pilot "buzzes" a house, a crowd, or some other object on the ground, at high speed. He pulls into a steep climb. During the ascent, the rotor begins to decelerate normally, since the propeller is partially relieving the rotor of the necessity of making lift; but at the top of the descent, as airspeed is rapidly being lost, the pilot pushes forward on the joystick and creates a condition of lessened G-loading (just as at the top of a roller coaster). The rotor decelerates, and so produces less drag, allowing the motor to thrust the aircraft nose-down. The rotor begins to flap wildly and in the process contacts the prop or the rudder. This maneuver has taken the lives of many high-time fixed-wing pilots, and not a few experienced gyrocopter pilots. The moral is obvious.

If you doubt the fact that a rotor needs a positive G-loading in order to autorotate, build yourself a balsa wood model and run around the living room a few times until you are convinced. An unloaded rotor won't autorotate.

Although negative-G maneuvers are also forbidden for helicopters, generally they are not as sensitive to zero-G flight as gyros. The reason being that power is supplied continuously to keep the rotor turning at all times. Nonetheless, maneuvers involving less than one G are best avoided in helicopters.

Porpoising

Poorly-trimmed gyros or helicopters can "hunt" up and down in high-speed forward flight. If the pilot's control response is not well ahead of the period of oscillation, the pitching may become divergent rapidly. That is to say, by improperly-timed control inputs the pilot can actually aggravate the hunting motion while trying to stop it. This is referred to as pilot-induced porpoising (PIP) or pilot-induced oscillation (PIO), and is extremely dangerous.

Porpoising is particularly dangerous in a gyrocopter, since zero-G conditions are often encountered at the top of the roller coaster ride. Factors which tend to precipitate incidents of porpoising are: pilot inexperience in type; wood rotorblades, insofar as they create a longer control lag; and lack of proper pitch trimming. As for the latter, it should be noted that most gyroplane designs (including all those ever given Type Certification by the CAA or FAA) incorporate some type of horizontal surface at the rear of the aircraft. Unfortunately, many pilots see this horizontal surface as some sort of rock guard or gravel deflector. In fact it serves a far more important function. Tervamaki in Finland and Barnett in the United States have studied pitch stability of light autogyros and conclude that modern-day gyrocopters have undesirable as well as dangerous flight characteristics at high speed in the absence of adequate stabilization about the pitch axis. Without either a horizontal fin on the tail or the gyroscopic stability of a rigid rotor, *all* rotorcraft are at best only marginally stable in the pitch axis.

Other Accidents

So far, little mention has been made of homebuilt helicopter accident statistics—for the simple reason that until recently, virtually no homebuilt helicopters flew on a regular basis, and thus, no accidents occurred. It has only been in the last half-dozen years or so that helicopter activity has mushroomed to its current status.

Some accidents have occurred, however: one resulting from tail rotor failure in flight; two due to loss of control in hover; one due to loss of rotor rpm; one due to hard landing following power-off autorotation.

Most rotorcraft accidents occur as the result of pilot error, as stated earlier. About 22% happen as the result of mechanical failure; the same, roughly, as for commercial rotorcraft. Of these, most are engine malfunction accidents, a comparatively small number resulting from airframe or rotor failure. Moreover, these accidents are almost never the fault of factory-supplied plans or components; instead, they are due to the use of substandard materials or an uncalled-for design change.

The use of substandard materials is encouraged by the startlingly high prices commanded by "aircraft quality" materials. After all, many people are originally attracted to homebuilt rotorcraft on the basis of low initial cost; some of these people cannot afford to fly any other way. Is it any surprise that the sport rotorcraft field even attracts people who cannot afford *quality* materials? Manufacturers have caught onto this and are becoming in some cases quite selective in whom they sell plans to.

The other major problem created by over-zealous amateurs is the one of design changes and substitutions. Curiously, although most people would not think of practicing law or medicine without a good deal of formal training, some amateurs feel confident they can engineer a better rotor, landing gear, or other system, than the highly-qualified man who designed these things in the first place. As a result, some people insist on "improving" an already-proven design without the slightest knowledge of stress, bending modes, or metallurgy. An example of this is that many beginners, thinking the 6061-T6 aluminum of which the Bensen B-8M is constructed to be too "weak," substitute a harder aluminum which then succumbs to fatigue far earlier. One man "strengthened" his gyrocopter to better withstand landing impacts by placing long braces running from axle to mast. These braces had the effect of transmitting landing shocks directly to the rotor head, resulting in early fatigue failure of the spindle bolt. Rather than build braces, this person would have been better off just letting some air out of his tires.

If you build a rotorcraft and wish to make a modification or in any way depart from the manufacturer's plans, check it out first with the FAA inspector or a factory representative. Most manufacturers will be glad to work with builders on design improvements. Don't go the cold-turkey route of designing and developing your own tail rotor, airframe, or main rotor. If you do, you could indeed wind up a cold turkey.

Information Is the Key

Fixed-wing pilots, constantly assailed by advisory circulars, airworthiness directives, articles, books, manuals, and brochures, are better educated in safe flight techniques than is generally admitted. The general aviation press and a handful of pilots' associations do a good job of keeping airplane owners advised of possible hazards to safe flight.

Sadly, such a cornucopia of information is, for the most part, unavailable to the owners and fliers of homebuilt rotorcraft. However, things are much better in this regard now than they were several years ago. The Popular Rotorcraft Association and its chapters have been extremely effective in educating rotorcraft owners in matters of safety. Manufacturers are also to be commended for their safety programs, as information dispersal assumes an important role in their overall efforts.

Now that sport rotorcraft enthusiasts are beginning to have access to information once so difficult to find, there is every reason to believe that the safety outlook for homebuilt rotorcraft is bright indeed.

Chapter 9
How to Fly in the Wind

As mentioned in the last chapter, one "ground proximity" type of accident which is frequent. Among homebuilt rotorcraft is the unsuccessful downwind turn. The reader is no doubt aware that this accident type claims fixed-wing victims as well. Nor are small rotorcraft alone involved; I have read of a $1,000,000-plus Sikorsky Skycrane biting the dust as a result of this type of mishap. Stacks of magazine articles have been written on the subject of "downwind turns." Why it persists as a major cause of accidents is anyone's guess.

There are basically two ways in which a rotorcraft pilot can get into trouble in a low-altitude downwind turn. One is to make an uncoordinated turn, following a semicircular path over the ground and as a result, losing airspeed. The other is to attempt the turn while flying with an engine that is producing enough power only for safe level flight. (In this case, the pilot should not be attempting any turns, let alone downwind turns!) Most authorities agree that downwind turns are safe so long as they are executed in such a way as to lose no airspeed during the turn. In practicality, this means that the pilot's eyes should be glued to the airspeed indicator before, during, and after the turn. In addition, the pilot must not forget to add power when entering a downwind turn, *as with any turn*. The steeper the turn, the more power. Finally, the turn should be coordinated by constant reference to the drift indicator or inclinometer, and not by reference to the ground. If these rules are followed, I will practically sign the guarantee that no accident will happen as a result of a "downwind turn."

It is important in rotorcraft flying to understand the confusions brought about by turning in the wind at low altitude. Our eyes are the major sense to interpret relative motion. Sure we have the semicircular canals in the ear that sense movement, but they do not override the eyes. In fact, we can become nauseated when our eyes tell a different story of motion. Have you ever been in a 360-degree movie dome? You know, the kind that gives such a real feeling of being immersed in the scene. The movie will often show a drive along a mountain road. In the darkened theater people "oh" and "ah" as they sway "against" the curves.

Birds seem to have built-in ways of sensing their rate of climb and sink, as well as direction, but we are creatures of the ground and are not equipped through evolution or ground-based experience to deal with the three-dimensional world of the air without special training and instruments.

Helicopters and gyroplanes fly slowly in relation to the wind and often turn low, so we base our actions by reference to the ground. This is often confusing.

Since the early days of flying when everyone stayed low, pilots found their airplanes seemed to handle differently, depending on whether they were turning into the wind or downwind. If a pilot were flying "against the wind" and turned to fly with the wind, the plane would drop, sometimes even hitting the ground. If a pilot turned toward the wind after flying downwind, the plan was "harder" to turn and easily gained altitude. It was obvious something must be happening because of the wind direction. Let's examine this problem in detail.

The Acceleration Theory

One explanation said that if you are flying 45 mph into a 15 mph wind, your ground speed is 30 mph, of course (45 mph flying speed minus the 15 mph headwind). When you turn downwind ground speed increases from 45 to 60 mph (45 plus 15)! To increase the speed of you and your airplane from 45 to 60 mph needs energy, which can only come from losing altitude or dropping, thus turning the height into speed. This sinking, explained the theory, is the danger of downwind turns. Pilots were cautioned to have extra speed and use special care to be a good 500 feet away from the ground before making a downwind turn. In the same way turning upwind resulted in a gain of energy as the ground speed slows from

45 mph to 30 mph so the plane can climb. The idea took hold because it seemed to square with our observations (Fig. 9-1).

But when flying higher, the phenomenon disappeared. At high altitude when circling in a strong wind, pilots could find not the slightest change in air speed or altitude.

Arguments raged on in print and hangar flying sessions. Fliers reasoned a rotorcraft is flying in the air at 45 mph no matter if its going into the wind or with the wind and its speed over the ground makes no difference. "oh, yeah," said the "Inertial Theorists." "Then how about a downwind landing across a ditch at 60 mph, compared to one upwind when the plane would hit at only 45 mph? Don't tell *us* ground speed isn't real."

To those trained in physics, however, the explanation is obvious. When the craft is in the air, the ground is not in the same system of reference.

Ground speed, in fact, does not make the slightest difference to the aircraft's inertia. Of course, if the plane touches the ground, how fast the plane is going in refernece to the ground *is* important

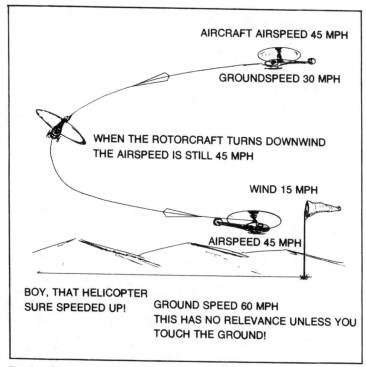

AIRCRAFT AIRSPEED 45 MPH

GROUNDSPEED 30 MPH

WHEN THE ROTORCRAFT TURNS DOWNWIND THE AIRSPEED IS STILL 45 MPH

WIND 15 MPH

AIRSPEED 45 MPH

BOY, THAT HELICOPTER SURE SPEEDED UP!

GROUND SPEED 60 MPH THIS HAS NO RELEVANCE UNLESS YOU TOUCH THE GROUND!

Fig. 9-1. Do you *really* gain speed in a downwind turn?

because the ground is now part of the system. The Inertial Theory was put to rest many years ago.

But a nagging doubt troubled even those fliers who found no changes in speed or altitude circling in the wind up high. When turns are done at low altitude, the plane does seem to handle differently as well as drop when turning downwind, even though we know the changes in ground speed have no affect.

The Wind Gradient

It was found that the wind is slower near the ground because of the drag of grass, bushes, and rough surface. "Aha," said pilots who found their airplanes dropping when they turned downwind. When turning downwind, if the plane drops into the slower air, its airspeed will increase since it has gained energy by flying into less "tail-wind."

It just isn't the cause of the problem. More important is our misreading of the relative movement of the ground.

Let's examine what your brain tells you in an upwind turn say, to the right. First, as you fly downwind, it seems you are going very fast because the ground is flowing quickly below. When you begin the turn, the ground seems to be slipping by from the right and the craft doesn't seem to be turning. As the rotorcraft keeps "sliding" sideways, it appears to be "slowing" because it is now heading upwind and its ground speed is less (Fig. 9-2).

Our brain interprets the change in speed as a reduction in the rate of turn so the pilot tries to turn harder to make it "get around." Close to the ground the pilot is reluctant to bank steeply so he skids to get the nose around. This can easily result in sinking due to high drag. The rotorcraft can even drop into the ground. It's not the "wind gradient," but the mind misreading the cues.

Now let's analyze the dreaded downwind turn (Fig. 9-3). As the rotor craft banks, the turn seems to accelerate in relation to the ground. Often, this sudden "speed up" and quick approach to our goal gives the impression that the rotorcraft is very easy to turn. In fact, if the turn is made with the normal control pressures and movement, the craft seems to be overbanking. You may subconsciously slow the craft and reduce the bank, but the rotorcraft slides too far away from its intended point. So now you must bank very steeply to tighten the turn to get it around to reach your goal. Low over the ground when it seems the craft is banking too much you tend to skid it around as well as banking more steeply (Fig. 9-4). Skidding and steepening the bank instantly raises the drag to put the

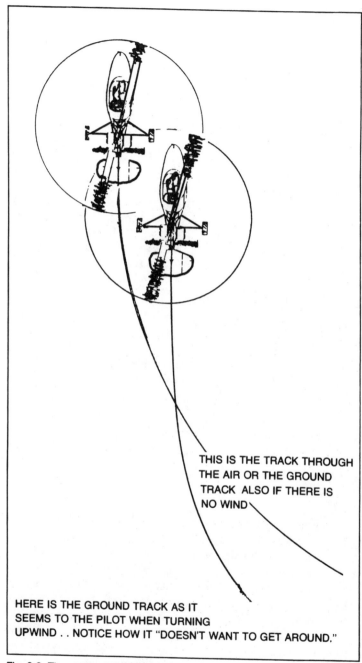

THIS IS THE TRACK THROUGH THE AIR OR THE GROUND TRACK ALSO IF THERE IS NO WIND

HERE IS THE GROUND TRACK AS IT SEEMS TO THE PILOT WHEN TURNING UPWIND . . NOTICE HOW IT "DOESN'T WANT TO GET AROUND."

Fig. 9-2. The problem of the upwind turn.

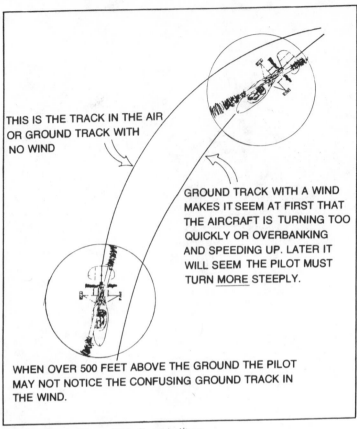

THIS IS THE TRACK IN THE AIR OR GROUND TRACK WITH NO WIND

GROUND TRACK WITH A WIND MAKES IT SEEM AT FIRST THAT THE AIRCRAFT IS TURNING TOO QUICKLY OR OVERBANKING AND SPEEDING UP. LATER IT WILL SEEM THE PILOT MUST TURN MORE STEEPLY.

WHEN OVER 500 FEET ABOVE THE GROUND THE PILOT MAY NOT NOTICE THE CONFUSING GROUND TRACK IN THE WIND.

Fig. 9-3. The problem of the downwind turn.

craft on the back side of the power curve. The result is often a disastrous settling to the ground.

What to Do?

The best way to deal with flying low in wind is: (1) Accept the fact that we aren't equipped to handle the situation, just as we are unable to fly in clouds using our senses without special instruments; (2) Decide your goal, such as the edge of the landing spot. Begin a turn you judge, from experience, that will be the proper bank to reach the goal and concentrate on airspeed and keeping the craft from slipping or skidding; (3) Look out at the ground momentarily.

Glances should be so brief that the movement of the ground does not confuse the brain. Eyes should be looking far out at the horizon and the instruments only. A good way to convince yourself is to do 360-degree turns in a strong wind at 100 feet without looking out. Then, try to do it looking at the ground (Fig. 9-5).

Wind Shear and Gusts

It is important in gusty air flying to be aware of the airspeed. If the rotorcraft accelerates but the airspeed drops, continue the acceleration by quickly increasing the throttle and/or putting the nose down. When the rotorcraft decelerates with the airspeed increasing, slow the throttle and pitch the nose up. Handling gusts and wind sheer is as simple as that; but to completely understand what's going on, let's look into the interesting mechanics of sudden changes in the wind (Fig. 9-6).

Back in the "Golden Age" of aviation in the 1930s, along with confusion about downwind turns, some pilots thought the inertia of the airplane was based on its ground speed. They said, for example, "A plane is on final at 35 mph with a headwind at 10 mph so its

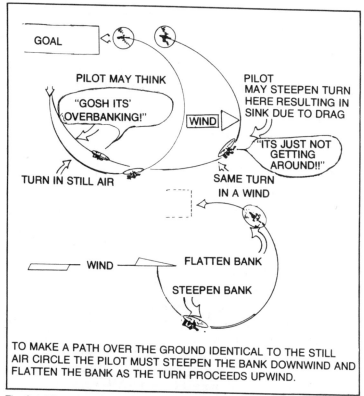

Fig. 9-4. Visual illusions in the downwind turn.

Fig. 9-5. Eyes on the airspeed in a low turn will keep you from being confused in a wind.

ground speed is 25 mph. If the wind stopped, the plane would be at 25 mph because its inertia is still there based on its ground speed." The pilot must add power and dive to regain the flying speed of 35 mph. Or, "If you were going to parachute from an airplane going 150 mph, you would feel a wind of 150 mph the instant you stepped out, at least until drag slowed you down, because your inertia is based on the 150 mph ground speed." What they didn't consider was the situation in winds. Say our plane is going 35 mph in still air. The ground speed is 35. A gust of 10 mph from behind will instantly drop the airspeed to 25 mph. The ground speed is still 35 mph but that has no meaning at all because the plane in the air needs 35 mph to fly so the pilot must push the nose down and increase the throttle. The pilot must remember the inertia of the airplane is in reference only to the system in which it is immersed, which is the air. Only when the plane touches another system, such as the ground, is the air-craft's speed relative to the new system. Here are a few of countless examples. Perhaps you can have fun discussing these situations with pilots who have not thought about them.

If a rotorcraft is going 50 mph in a 40 mph wind, the ground speed is 10 mph. If it hits something attached to the ground, such as a kite, tree, or hill, it will bump at 10 mph because its ground speed is important whenever the ground is touched. If it hits a balloon floating in the air, it will strike with its air inertia of 50 mph, since they're both in the same reference system. In the air, the ground speed has nothing to do with the plane's inertia.

To help understand systems let's look at some everyday experiences. Picture a person running on one of the moving sidewalks at a big airport. Running with the sidewalk the speeds are added but only in reference to something *not* on the treadmill. Likewise, going against the treadmill the speed of the walkway is subtracted from your running speed. If you're going 10 mph on a walkway going 10 mph, you will bump someone on the walkway standing still at 10 mph. If someone not on the walkway leaned over and you bumped that person, the blow would be at 20 mph because that person is out of your system of reference. If you're going *against* the walkway at 11 mph, your speed if you bumped that same person, would only be 1 mph. If a person going with the walkway at 10 mph stepped off, the immediate speed would be 20 mph which might be dangerous to bystanders, but if the person ran 20 mph against the walkway, only 10 mph would be the speed leaving the end and the person would

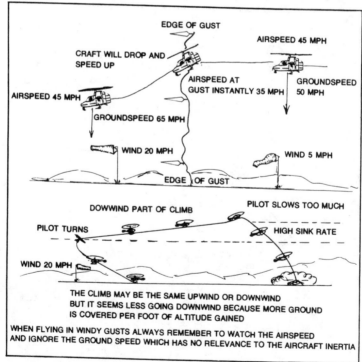

Fig. 9-6. Flying in windy gusts.

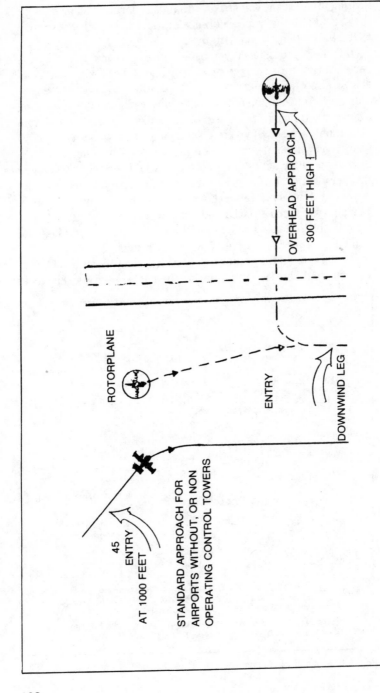

ROTORPLANE

ENTRY

OVERHEAD APPROACH
300 FEET HIGH

DOWNWIND LEG

45
ENTRY
AT 1000 FEET

STANDARD APPROACH FOR
AIRPORTS WITHOUT, OR NON
OPERATING CONTROL TOWERS

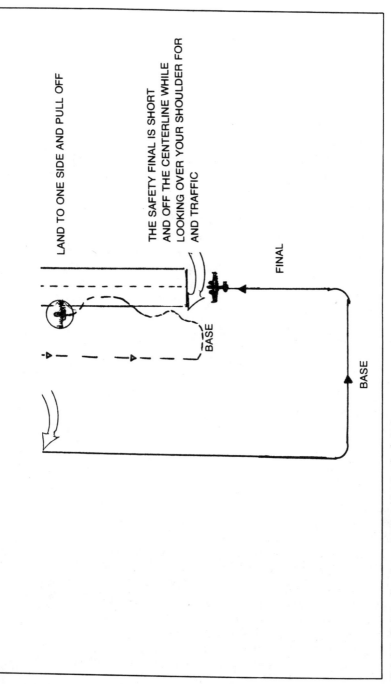

LAND TO ONE SIDE AND PULL OFF

THE SAFETY FINAL IS SHORT
AND OFF THE CENTERLINE WHILE
LOOKING OVER YOUR SHOULDER FOR
AND TRAFFIC

FINAL

BASE

BASE

Fig. 9-7. Rotorcraft pattern compared to standard airplanes.

have to push his legs hard and accelerate strongly to reach his 20 mph pace.

So what does this mean to aircraft? It must be understood that ground speed has nothing to do with the action of the craft in the air. An aircraft is affected only by the air. It's as if the earth did not exist. The airspeed is the thing to watch because the pressure of the air on the rotor and control surfaces tells you how to fly for proper control. Watch the airspeed in windy air, stand up and shout it, fix it in your sub, semi and full consciousness. *Watch the airspeed!*

More examples: Say you're heading for the old landing patch and a gust hits from behind (or a lull from the wind in front, it's all the same); your airspeed is whatever the gust has subtracted from your speed. If you are going 30 mph, rear gust at 15 mph makes the airspeed 15 mph. The plane will pitch down, assuming it's properly designed and balanced. Since the speed has been cut in half, drag has been reduced four times, so it will dive and pick up speed quickly. You feel an acceleration and see the ground coming up. An inexperienced seat-of-the-pants pilot would probably pull up as automatically as a sneeze. The rotorcraft drops more as airspeed (and therefore lift) is even less. Now the ground is very close and our inexperienced pilot is too low off the end of the landing spot so, of course, noses up even more. Smack! The machine is sitting in the bushes short of the landing spot. With last minute added power, the craft may still drop because it's in a high drag attitude called the "back side of the power curve." (Big jets are particularly susceptible to these wind sheer gust incidences because a jet engine takes six to eight seconds from throttle advance to give thrust. The big plane has wheels and flaps down and will not accelerate quickly even when the power finally does come.)

In gusty weather, watch the airspeed and use the seat-of-the-pants feelings and react this way: (1) When you feel the rotorcraft speed up, continue the acceleration by adding power or nosing down. It means a gust has come from behind or the wind has quit. If you looked at the airspeed, you would see it had dropped. (2) When you feel yourself suddenly slow it indicates a gust from the front, or the tail wind has stopped. To continue the path you wish, throttle back to continue to slow down. The sensation of slowing means the plane has hit a gust from in front, greatly raising its drag; the nose will try to pitch up and the airspeed will have increased.

It's perfectly safe to land at airports without control towers if you do not bother or conflict with the regular airplanes. The standard pattern for lightplanes is a box with all turns to the left with one

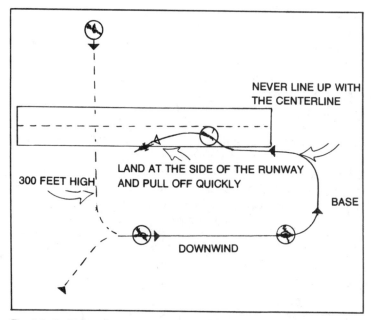

NEVER LINE UP WITH
THE CENTERLINE

LAND AT THE SIDE OF THE RUNWAY
AND PULL OFF QUICKLY

300 FEET HIGH

BASE

DOWNWIND

Fig. 9-8. Typical rotorcraft approach and landing.

edge over the runway nearest facing the wind. Entry into this pattern calls for a 45 degree turn into the downwind leg at 1000 feet with spacing between airplanes maintained by slowing down if too close to the plane ahead or speeding up if someone is too close to your tail. A slow rotorcraft would be in conflict if it tried using the standard pattern mixed in with fast airplanes. You could follow the airport's helicopter pattern if you knew what it was for each airport, but lacking that, make a pattern similar to the other planes (Figs. 9-7 through 9-9).

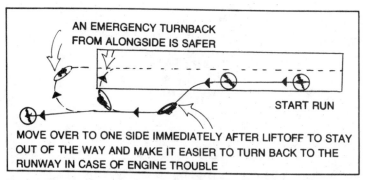

AN EMERGENCY TURNBACK
FROM ALONGSIDE IS SAFER

START RUN

MOVE OVER TO ONE SIDE IMMEDIATELY AFTER LIFTOFF TO STAY OUT OF THE WAY AND MAKE IT EASIER TO TURN BACK TO THE RUNWAY IN CASE OF ENGINE TROUBLE

Fig. 9-9. Typical takeoff at an uncontrolled airfield planned for safety.

111

This approach will look the same but, in fact, will be quite different. The pattern should be lower and smaller than that of the regular planes. Stay at about 300 feet as you enter downwind leg and 100 feet to one side of the runway you intend to land on, called the "active." Check ahead for planes on base or turning to final and especially try to look far ahead for someone on a long final. If everything is all clear, turn a short base over the end of the runway to final. Stay alongside the active runway until about 10 feet up. Check again for landing traffic, move over to the edge of the runway, and land on the side. As soon as you are slow, pull off the runway and taxi to wherever you plan to park, get fuel, etc.

By making your pattern inside and lower than the other planes, you are always where they can see you. Yet, the pattern is similar to the regular planes so they know you are approaching to land.

Chapter 10
Clubs and Supplies

The sport of rotorcraft flying is unique in the world of aviation so most enthusiasts join with others to share progress in design and good building and flying techniques (Fig. 10-1). There are two organizations you may join.

Marty Hollman has founded the Gyroplane Association International with clubs on many of the continents. His address is 11082 Bel Aire Court., Cupertino, CA 95014. The chapter in Europe is contacted by Helge Svensson, Annebergvagen 12, S 13668 Handen, Sweden. In England, it's John Kitchin, High Street Farm, Boxford, Newbury, Berkshire RG16 8DD, England.

In the USA the Popular Rotorcraft Association was founded in 1963 and now has 56 chapters and a bi-monthly magazine. They have many local activities and fly-ins as well as a national convention. The chapters have training equipment and qualified instructor pilots to help beginners learn to fly rotarywing aircraft safely. Membership is now $18 annually which includes the magazine, membership card and discounted patches, caps and technical books. The address is P.O. Box 570, Stanton, CA 90680

Popular Rotorcraft Association Chapters

Southern California Rotorcraft Association
Ken Brock, 11852 Western, Stanton, CA 90680

Tidewater Rotorcraft Club
Gene Sawyer, 5117 Bennett's Pasture Road, Suffolk, VA 23434

West Penn Rotorcraft Club, Inc.
Helen Darvassy, P.O. Box 882, Oil City, PA 16301

Fig. 10-1. Homebuilt rotorcraft have been built worldwide. Mr. Kawachi of Japan built this one.

Northern California Rotorcraft Club
Ric Jesch, 1919 - 7th Street, Berkeley, CA 94710

Toronto Rotorcraft Club, Inc.
Jerry Forest, 53 Hamptonbrook Drive, Weston, Ont. M9P 1A2

Minnesota Rotorcraft Club
Bob Tozer, 8330 Fairfield Road, Brooklyn Park, MN 55544

Greater Midwest Chapter
Dick Wunderlich, 1504 Connor Avenue, Lockport, IL 60441

Badger Minichoppers
Warren Lueders, 20625 Brook Park Drive, Waukesha, WI 53186

Sunstate Rotor Club, Inc.
Slim Rosenberger, 6401 North Coolidge Avenue, Tampa, FL 33614

Golden Horseshoe Rotorcraft Assn., Inc.
August Carlow, RR 1, Mt. Pleasant, Ontario N0E 1K0, Canada

Western Washington Rotorcraft Club
Henry Abbott, P.O. Box 385, RD 1, Enumclaw, WA 98022

San Diego County Gyrocopter Club, Inc.
Jack Sievers, 5345 El Noche Way, San Diego, CA 92124

Michigan Rotorcraft Club
Jack Lohr, 36345 Briarcliff, Sterling Heights, MI 48077

Indiana Rotorcraft Assn., Inc.
122 Garfield Drive, Greenfield, IN 46140

St. Louis Rotorcraft Club
Willard Meyer, 405 Meyer Drive, Kirkwood, MO 63122

Cincinnati Rotorcraft Club
Ed Alderfer, 4278 Shafor Drive, Hamilton, OH 45011

Blueridge Rotorcraft Club (SW Virginia & East. Tenn.)
Paul Brown, P.O. Box 416, Honaker, VA 24260

South Bay Rotorcraft Club
Leo Riley, 513 North Guadalupe, Redondo Beach, CA 90277

Alabama Area
Carl Freeman, 1520 Terrell Road, Mobile, AL 36601

Western New York Rotorcraft Club
Russell Brown, Murphy Hill Road, Horseheads, NY

Rotor Rooters
Martha Reddinger, 44277 North Carolside Avenue, Lancaster, CA 93534

Top of Illinois Gyronauts
Fran Jansen, Ridott, IL 61067

Tri-State Rotorcraft Club
Frank Polston, 714—38th Street, Cairo, IL 62914

East Texas Rotorcraft Club
Edy Demague, Rt. 3, P.O. Box 291A, Mt. Pleasant, TX 75455

Mid-Missouri Rotorcraft Club
c/o Ferdinand G. A. Telle, 111, 712 West Salem Avenue, Rolla, MO 65401

Central Valley Rotorcraft Club
Alan Tatarian, 725 North Bush, Fresno, CA 93727

Peach State Rotorcraft Club
Chuck Nickerson, 2138 Gunstock Drive, Stone Mountain, GA 30087

Instruction, Plans, Kits, and Supplies

Eastern Bensen Gyrocopters, Inc.
Richmond Airport
West Kingston, RI 02892
Telephone: (401) 783-1498

C. "Jack" Gordon has the Bensen Kit, parts, plans, and materials as well as the Menzie Muffler System. The company sells Ken Brock's custom accessories also. Jack gives demonstrations and flight instruction by appointment.

Bob Nesbit's Gyrocopter Sales
8908 Nightingale Lane
Pineville, NC 28134
Telephone: (704) 542-1880
Bob specializes in Magneto repair and has plans, kits, and materials for the Bensen, as well as offering dual instruction.

Clinton Rotor-Craft Company
George J. Charlet
P.O. Box 267
Clinton, LA 70722
Telephone: (504) 683-5432
George gives dual seat instruction and demonstrations. He has the Bensen dealership for plans and kits in Louisiana.

Harry Cordon
8225 Asher Avenue
Little Rock, AR 72204
Telephone: (501) 565-4952
Harry is the Bensen dealer in Arkansas and can furnish plans, kits, parts, and instruction.

Ron Menzie
Star Route 3
Beebe, AR 72012
Telephone: (501) 882-6112
Another Bensen dealer in Arkansas whose specialty is the Menzie McCulloch Muffler System

Ken Brock Manufacturing
11852-P Western Avenue
Stanton, CA 90680
Telephone: (714) 898-4366
Ken Brock has a training program he conducts at El Mirage Dry Lake, as well as a complete line of kits, plans, and parts for his KB-2 gyroplane.

R & D Aeronautical Engineering Co., Inc.
P.O. Box 1108
Plano, TX 75074
Telephone: (214) 442-2294

This company specializes in the McCulloch gyroplane two-cycle engines and a catalogue of other supplies.

Dick Wunderlich Gyrocopter
1504 Conner Avenue
Lockport, IL 60441
Telephone: (815) 835-5833
Dick has a flexible shaft pre-rotator to enable a gyroplane to take off from anyplace it can safely land. He also furnishes rotor tachmometers, rotor brakes, and instrument panels.

Telle Rotorcraft
712 West Salem Avenue
Rolla, MO 65401
Telephone: (314) 364-3376
Ferdinand Telle has a machine shop to service and remanufacture Volkswagen air-cooled engines for airboats, aircraft, and gyroplanes. He makes a 10-foot long, 7-inch chord flush riveted rotor blade for gyroplanes and helicopters as well as the rotor hubs and heads.

Rotor Hawk Industries Corp.
P.O. Box 856
Green Cove Springs, FL 3043
Telephone: (904) 284-7179
Rotor Hawk specializes in all-aluminum, flush riveted 10 and 12 foot blades of 8¼ inch chord and a 34 inch adjustable hub.

Rotordyne Company
1006 West Oak
Burbank, CA 91506
Telephone: (213) 849-4782
This company has a catalogue listing the many components for gyroplanes such as, McCulloch engines and certified materials. They are most noted for their aluminum bonded rotor blades at $550.

Winther-Hollmann Aircraft, Inc.
11082 Bel Aire Court
Cupertino, CA 95014
Telephone: (408) 255-2194
Marty Hollmann has developed a high performance laminar flow composite construction blade for $1250 complete with adjustable rub. His company also sells plans for the HA-2M Sportster, two-seater gyroplane; John Bond Sky Dancer; Barnet J4B.

RotorWay Aircraft Inc.
14805 South Interstate 10
Tempe, AZ 85284

"Date" Secor
13209 North Neiff Road
Clio, MI 48420
Mr. Secor has Teardrop fiberglass wheel pants for the standard Bensen or Brock axles. They sell for $90 a pair including hardware.

Barnett Rotorcraft
4307 Olivehurst Avenue
Olivehurst, CA 95961
Jerrie Barnett sells plans for his gyroplane J4B and is working on a two-place version which may be ready soon.

International Helicopters, Inc.
P.O. Box 107
Maryville, NY 14757
Telephone: 753-2113
Bob Dart manufacturers and sells kits and plans for the Commuter helicopter.

Tech Man Company
8525 East Duarte Road
San Gabriel, CA 92775
Telephone: (213) 286-2235
Jim Eich has plans and descriptive text with photographs of his JE-2 two-place gyroplane, using an engine in front and tandem seating, for $100.

Bensen
P.O. Box 31047
Raleigh, NC 27622
Telephone: (919) 787-4224 and 787-4264
Igor Bensen has a complete catalogue of every part needed to make his gyrocopter from plans as well as complete kits ready to assemble. They are worldwide dealers for his products and, of course, training and materials available from them too.

Trailers

Trailers for Homebuilt Gyroplanes, or anything else that will fit, can be had from Gunter's, P.O. Box 160, Port Neches, TX 77651. Plans $50, ready-made $900.

Index